Britain's Best Football Grounds
from the air

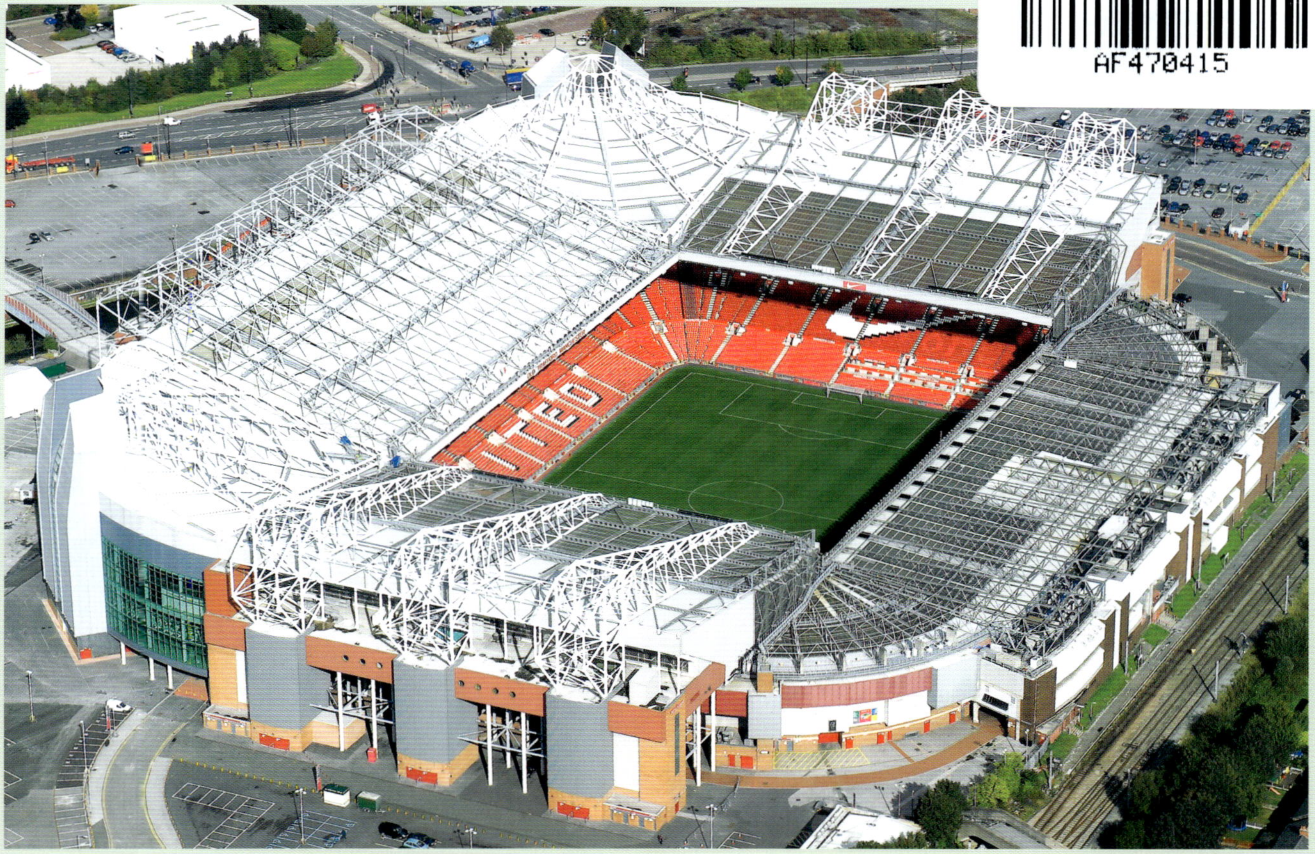

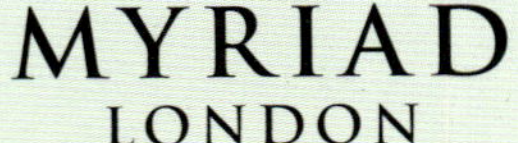

Arsenal started life as a team called Dial Square in 1886, based in Woolwich, south-east London. They changed their name to Royal Arsenal in 1887 and to Woolwich Arsenal in 1891. Their early games were played on Woolwich Common but they moved to Manor Field in 1888, where they remained for the next 26 years. Despite being successful in the League, which they joined in 1893, their gates were low and they went into voluntary liquidation in 1910. Henry Norris, owner of Fulham FC, bought the struggling club and moved them to Highbury, north London, in 1913 much to the annoyance of their neighbours Spurs and Clapton Orient. After the First World War, Arsenal rejoined the First Division where they have remained since 1919. Architect Claude Waterlow Ferrier was commissioned to design a stadium for Arsenal, and he set about using an Art Deco style for the ground. In 1931 he extended the terraces at each end and began building the West Stand. The 1930s also saw success on the pitch: Arsenal won the League five times and the FA Cup twice. In 1935 an AFC monogrammed roof was added to the Laundry End Terrace; in the same season the club recorded its highest attendance when 73,295 turned out to see Arsenal take on Sunderland. In 1936 the East Stand was replaced and looked almost identical to Ferrier's West Stand. The 1970s saw more seats installed at Highbury, and further developments came in the 1980s when the club added executive boxes to the Clock End. In 1991 the club drew up plans to rebuild the new North Stand in order to increase capacity. The club had to play in front of just three stands in the 1992-93 season as the bulldozers moved in and a mural took the place of the fans on the North Bank. The new two-tiered North Stand opened in 1993. The Clock End and the East and West Terraces were next to be developed bringing a total capacity of 38,500 all-seated. In February 2004 Arsenal began building a 60,000 all-seater stadium just five minutes from Highbury at Ashburton Grove on the site of a disused railway goods yard. At the beginning of the 2006-7 season Arsenal moved into the new Emirates Stadium.

Ground: Emirates Stadium

Capacity: 60,432

Record attendance: (at Highbury) 73,295 vs Sunderland, March 9 1935

Record attendance: (at the Emirates) 60.132 vs Reading, March 3 2007

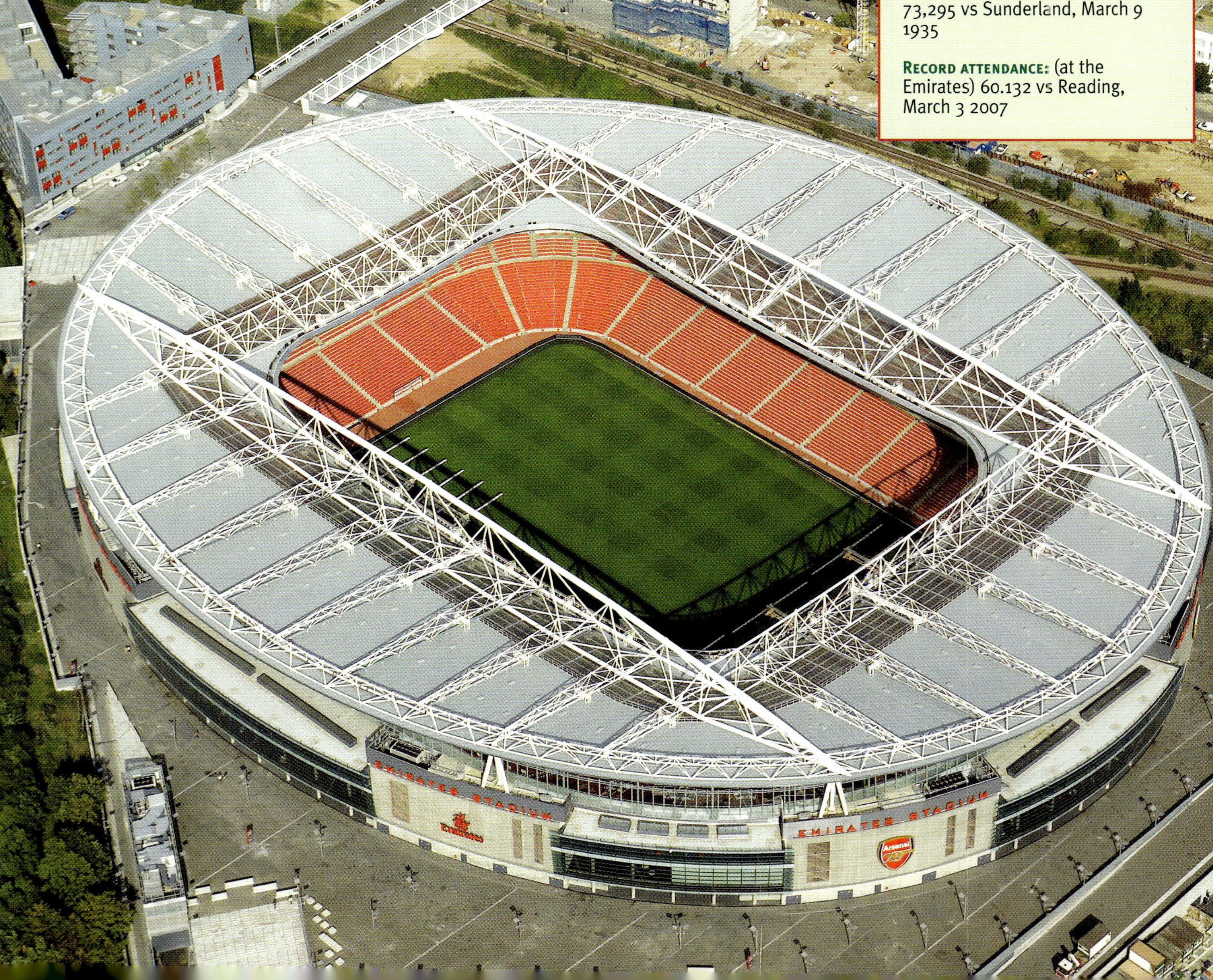

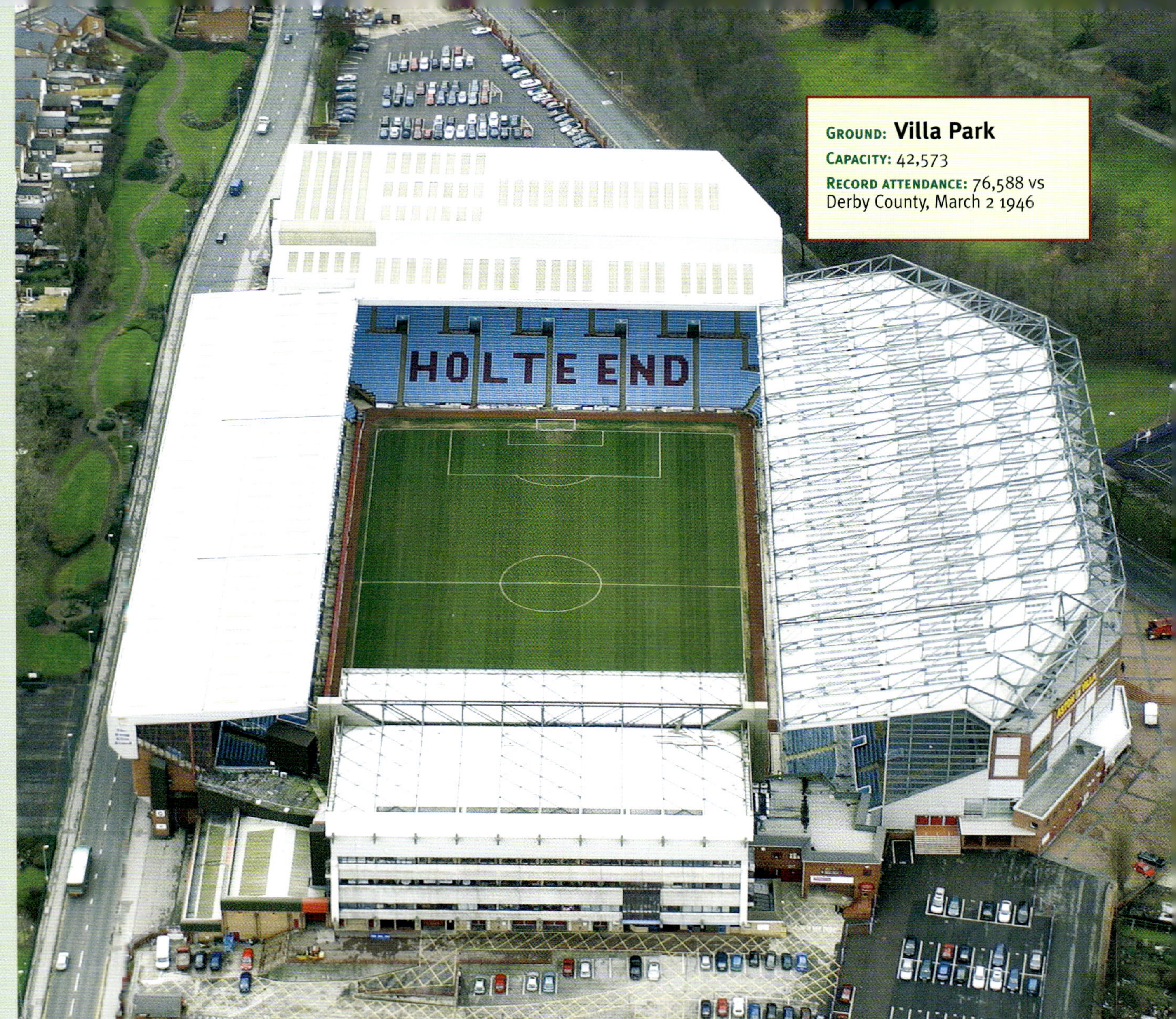

GROUND: Villa Park
CAPACITY: 42,573
RECORD ATTENDANCE: 76,588 vs Derby County, March 2 1946

Aston Villa was formed by members of the Villa Cross Wesleyan Chapel in 1874. The club moved to the Aston Lower grounds in 1896 after spending 20 years at a basic ground on Wellington Road. The site was a leisure park dating back to the 1870s but had fallen into a state of disrepair. Villa began developing the ground, building a main stand on what had been a sub-tropical garden. Banking was raised on the other three sides of the ground and a basic barrel roof was added to the Trinity Road side. The ground opened in 1897, the same year Villa won the League and Cup double. Attendances continued to rise and prior to the First World War Villa were drawing in regular crowds of 26,000. In 1914 Villa realised their plans for future development of the ground. The work began with the removal of the concrete cycle path, which had run around the pitch; both end terraces were banked and another terrace added to the front of the Witton Lane Stand. After the war the Trinity Road Stand was built, a stand which was so extravagant in design it cost the club £89,810. The Holte End was extended during the Second World War and in 1946 Villa Park saw its highest ever crowd of 76,588. Villa Park's selection as a location for World Cup games brought about further developments with seats being added to the ground's terracing. The two-tiered North Stand was built in 1977, with further developments coming in the light of the Taylor report. In 1990 the Holte End terracing was updated and the roof extended but as a result of poor planning the whole structure had to be demolished in 1994 and replaced with a two-tier stand. Trinity Road Stand was refurbished in time for the 1996 European Championships. In order to maintain a capacity in excess of 40,000 the club set about planning to redevelop the Witton Lane Stand (now the Doug Ellis Stand). There are plans to re-develop and enlarge the North Stand, extending and filling in the open corners to bring total stadium capacity at Villa Park to 50,000 plus.

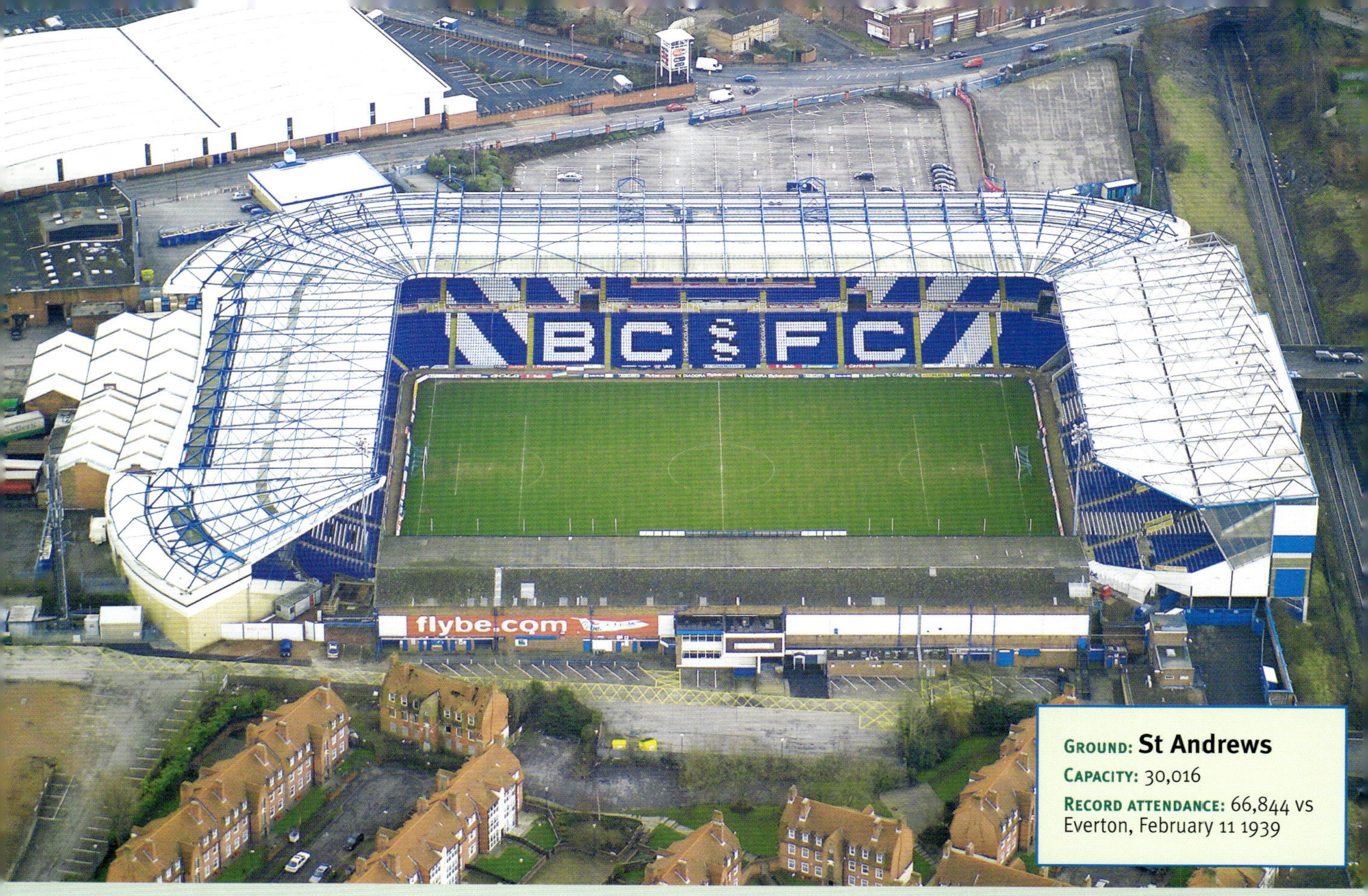

GROUND: St Andrews
CAPACITY: 30,016
RECORD ATTENDANCE: 66,844 vs Everton, February 11 1939

Birmingham City started as the Small Heath Alliance in 1875. Their first pitch was on waste ground on Arthur Street but as their fan base grew, they moved to Muntz Street, remaining there for 29 years. They turned professional in 1885 and in 1905 became Birmingham FC. The Blues moved to St Andrews in 1906. A Main Stand and a Kop terrace, with a capacity of 48,000, were built. During the Second World War the ground was damaged by bombs over 20 times and the Main Stand burned down. The club had to move, first to Leamington and then to Villa Park until 1943, while their ground was repaired. They emerged from the war with a new name, Birmingham City FC. The Kop reopened in 1947 and a new two-tiered Main Stand opened in 1954. Success in Europe funded the building of the Railway End Stand in 1963-4. In March 1993 David Sullivan took over and drew up plans for a £4.5m development of the Kop and Tilton Road End, which opened in 1994; in 1999 the Railway End was redeveloped.

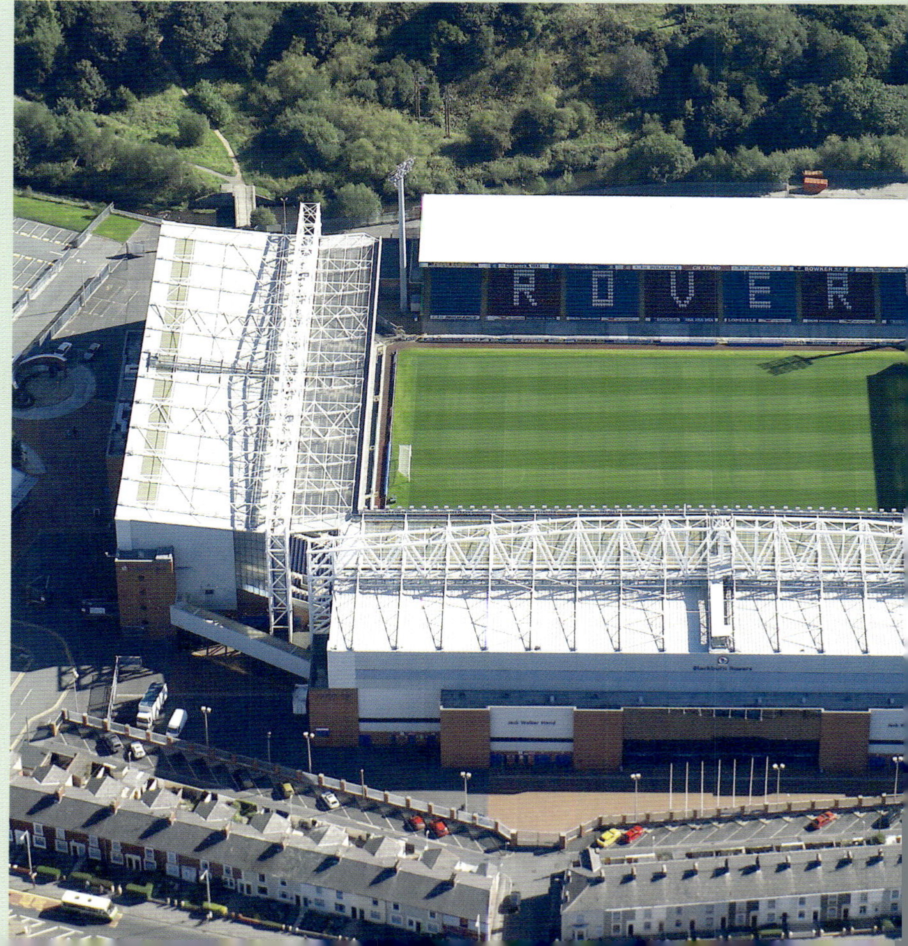

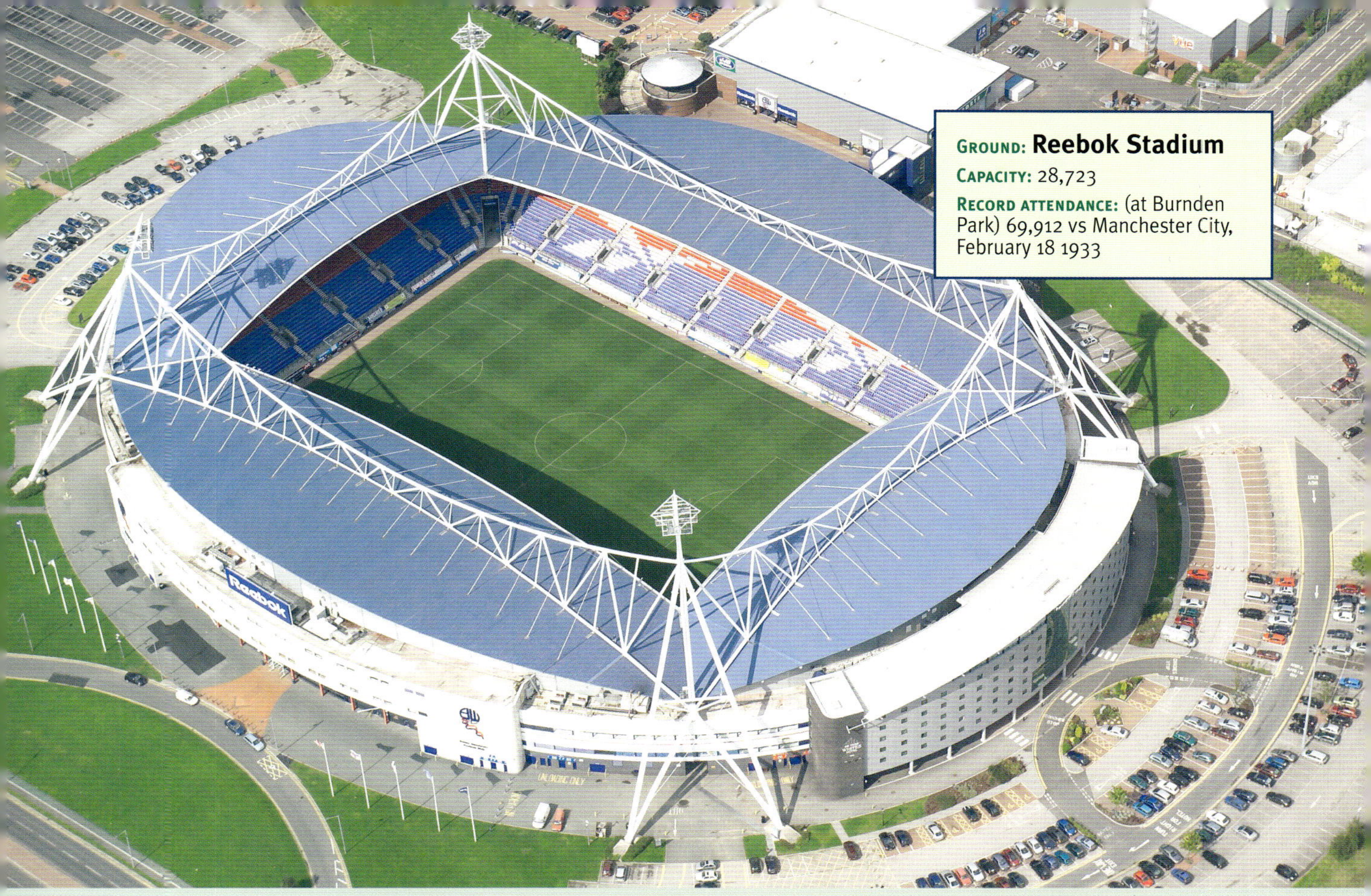

Ground: Reebok Stadium
Capacity: 28,723
Record attendance: (at Burnden Park) 69,912 vs Manchester City, February 18 1933

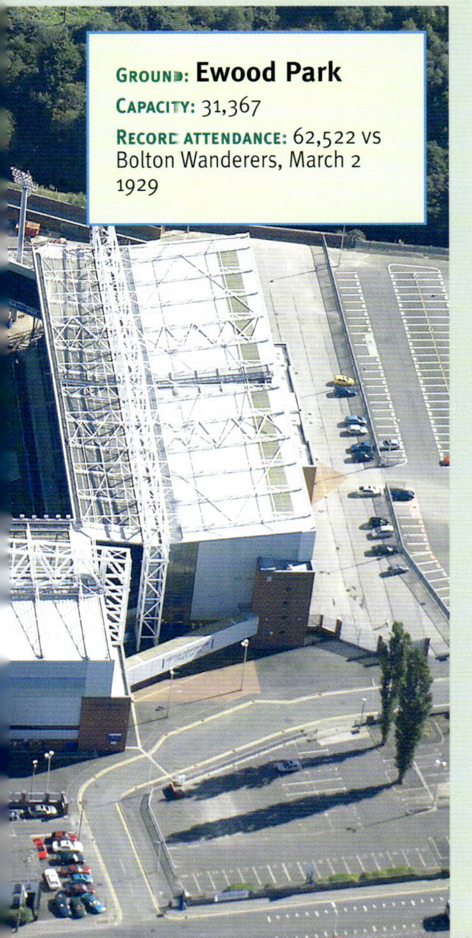

Ground: Ewood Park
Capacity: 31,367
Record attendance: 62,522 vs Bolton Wanderers, March 2 1929

Blackburn Rovers was formed in 1875. It took the club a year before they settled at their first ground, Oozehead. They moved a further four times before settling at Ewood Park in 1890. In 1905 Laurence Cotton, a textile baron, set about transforming the ground. Between 1905-1914 he spent £33,000 on ground improvements. First came a pitched roof on the Darwen End, followed by the building of the Main Stand and the Nuttall Street Stand. Further improvements in 1914 came after Rovers had won the League title, when the Riverside Stand was built. By 1913 the capacity was 70,866. In 1980 safety regulations brought the capacity at Ewood Park down to 23,400. In 1987 Chairman Bill Fox persuaded his friend, Jack Walker, to help rebuild the Riverside Stand. In 1991 Walker set about transforming the club. He spent £13m on the team in 18 months and drew up plans for the building of three two-tiered stands. The Jack Walker Stand was opened in November 1994.

Bolton Wanderers started as a Sunday school team called Christ Church FC, playing on Park Recreation Ground. They moved to Dick Cockle's Field on Pikes Lane in 1877 but left to become Bolton Wanderers. In 1881 they moved to a proper sports ground on Pikes Lane. In 1893 rising rents led Wanderers to bid farewell to Pikes Lane and build a new ground, Burnden Park, which was home to the Trotters for 102 years. The club's first attempt at winning the FA Cup came in 1904 and despite losing, the money raised meant they could build a main stand and terrace and cover the Great Lever End. The 1920s saw three FA Cup wins for Bolton, and again more ground improvements followed with the new Burnden Stand. The 1980s were the next major period of change for the club. Crowds dropped to an all-time low of 2,902. By the 1990s, Bolton's fortunes had reversed; they reached the Premiership in 1995 and moved into the impressive Reebok Stadium which opened in 1997.

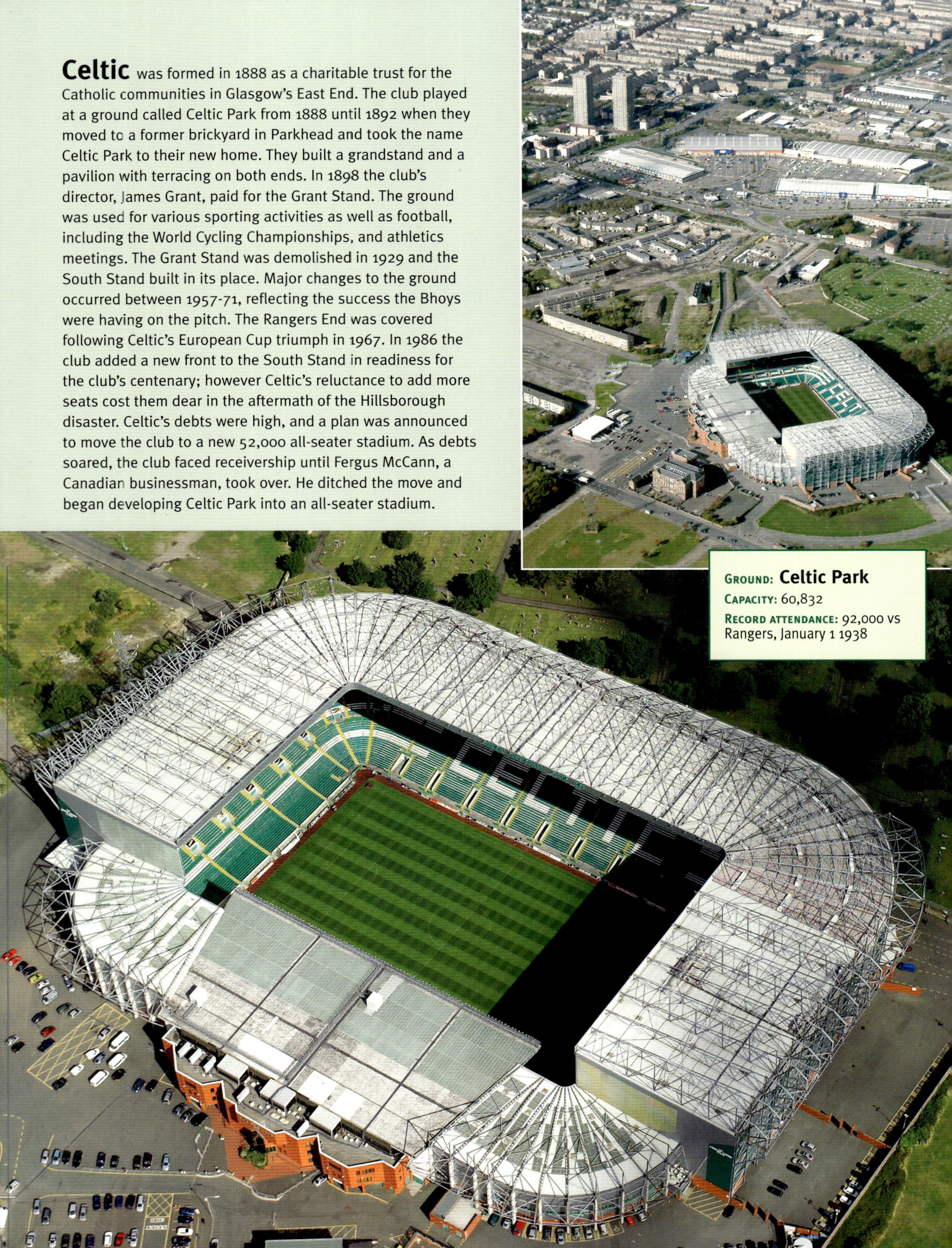

Celtic was formed in 1888 as a charitable trust for the Catholic communities in Glasgow's East End. The club played at a ground called Celtic Park from 1888 until 1892 when they moved to a former brickyard in Parkhead and took the name Celtic Park to their new home. They built a grandstand and a pavilion with terracing on both ends. In 1898 the club's director, James Grant, paid for the Grant Stand. The ground was used for various sporting activities as well as football, including the World Cycling Championships, and athletics meetings. The Grant Stand was demolished in 1929 and the South Stand built in its place. Major changes to the ground occurred between 1957-71, reflecting the success the Bhoys were having on the pitch. The Rangers End was covered following Celtic's European Cup triumph in 1967. In 1986 the club added a new front to the South Stand in readiness for the club's centenary; however Celtic's reluctance to add more seats cost them dear in the aftermath of the Hillsborough disaster. Celtic's debts were high, and a plan was announced to move the club to a new 52,000 all-seater stadium. As debts soared, the club faced receivership until Fergus McCann, a Canadian businessman, took over. He ditched the move and began developing Celtic Park into an all-seater stadium.

GROUND: Celtic Park
CAPACITY: 60,832
RECORD ATTENDANCE: 92,000 vs Rangers, January 1 1938

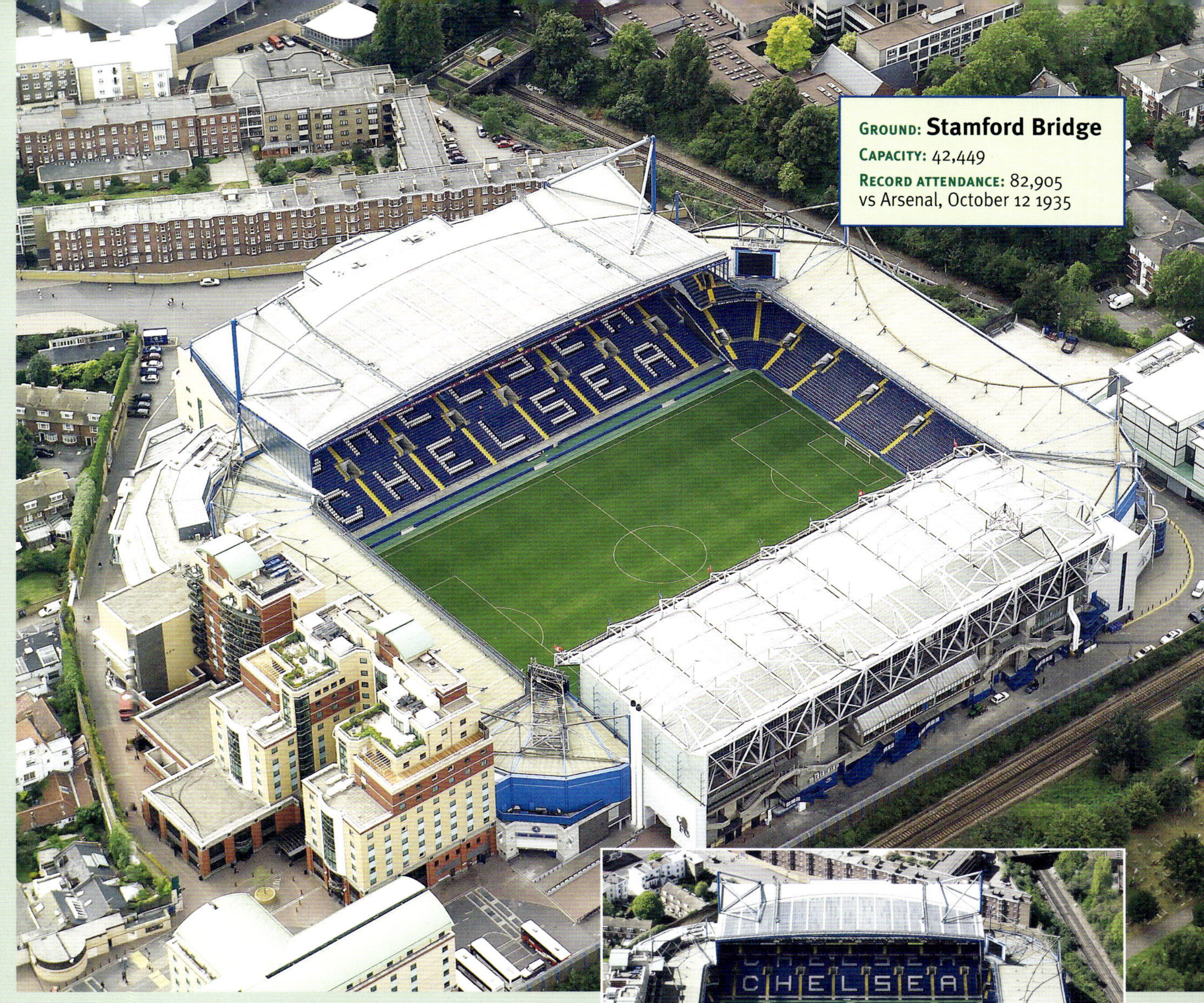

Ground: Stamford Bridge
Capacity: 42,449
Record attendance: 82,905 vs Arsenal, October 12 1935

Chelsea was formed in 1905 but their ground, Stamford Bridge, came into being almost 30 years earlier in 1877, when the London Athletic Club developed it as a running track from an orchard and market garden. In 1904 Gus Mears took over the ownership of the ground and developed it into a venue for cycling, athletics and football. Mears commissioned the Scottish architect, Archibald Leitch, to design the 5,000-seater Main Stand. Mears and his friend Fred Parker established Chelsea FC in 1905. Chelsea had a remarkably successful first season and by 1907 their promotion to the First Division saw them attracting the highest gates in the League. Despite staging FA Cup finals and other sporting events, the club did not invest much money in the ground. It was not until 1935 that a cover was added to the Fulham Road Terrace. In 1939 a 2,500-seater stand was erected on the north-east corner, on stilts above the terracing. A new north stand was opened in 1945, but it was during the 1960s and 1970s when major developments took place at the Bridge. At the time the West Stand was built, the team were going through one of their most successful periods ever, winning the League Cup in 1965 and the FA Cup in 1970. They also won the European Cup Winners' Cup in 1971. In 1971 plans were drawn up for the three-tier East Stand, the first stand in the £5.5m development. The Stand opened in 1974, but Chelsea's luck took a turn for the worse. They were heavily in debt, they were relegated to the Second Division and gates were dropping. In the 1982-83 season gates twice dropped to below 7,000. It was in this season that Ken Bates took over as chairman. Over the following 20 years, Chelsea Village was developed. Two new all-seater stands were built at each end and corner stands added. In 2001 the West Stand was rebuilt, a two-tiered stand bringing capacity up to 42,449.

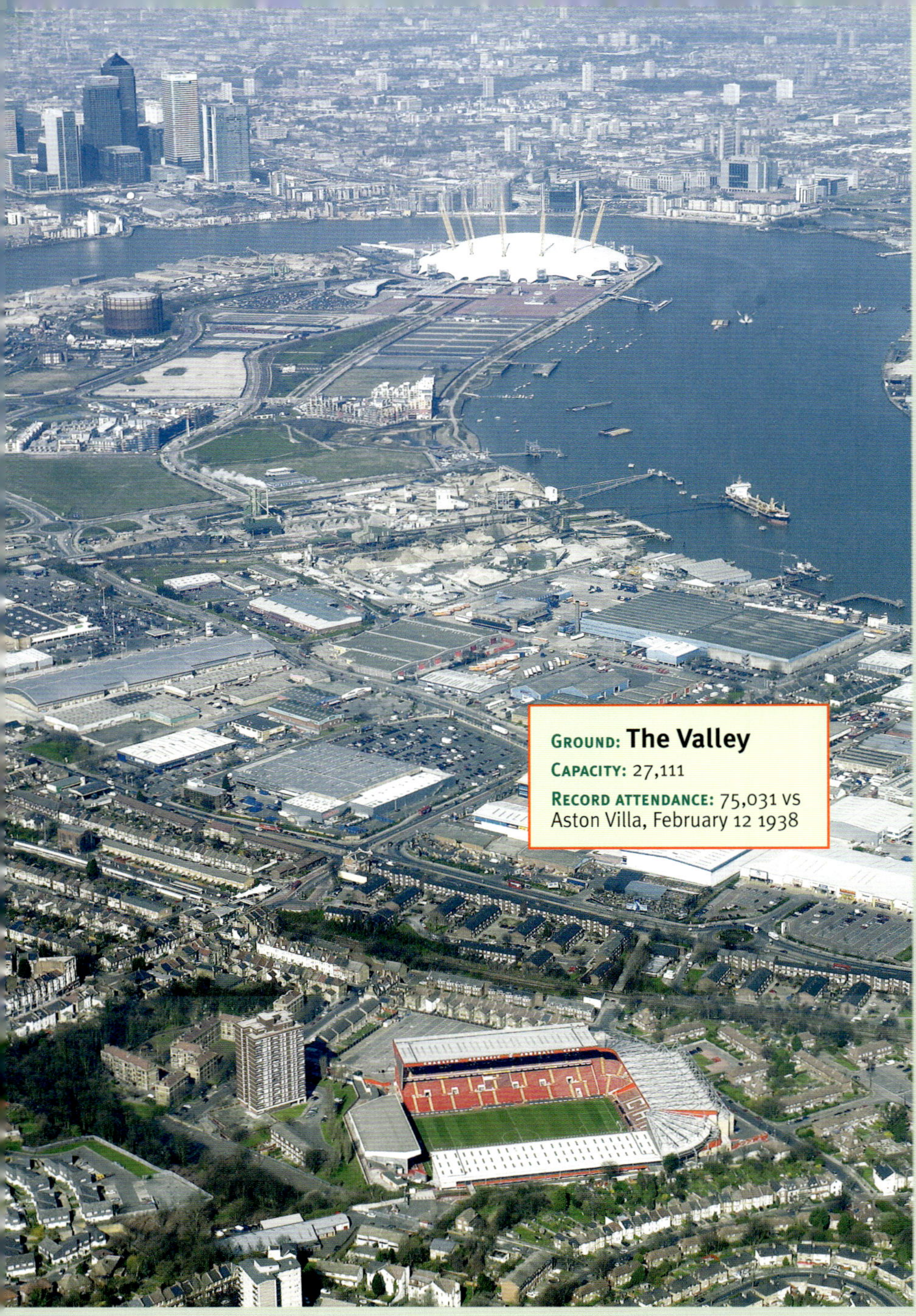

GROUND: The Valley

CAPACITY: 27,111

RECORD ATTENDANCE: 75,031 vs Aston Villa, February 12 1938

Charlton Athletic

Charlton Athletic was formed in 1905 and played at four grounds before arriving at The Valley in 1919. At the time The Valley was a chalk and sand pit known as "the swamp". By 1921 the club had turned professional and built the Main Stand on the west side of the pitch; the ground was famed for its vast East Terrace. In 1923 the club left The Valley and moved to a ground called The Mount, returning after just one season. The club had run up huge debts and were facing a bleak future until the Gliksten brothers stepped in with a £100,000 rescue package in 1931. In 1985, poor financial decisions meant Charlton had to leave The Valley and move in with local rivals Crystal Palace; they did not return to The Valley until 1992, following a campaign by fans to persuade Greenwich Council to allow them to develop their old ground. The Valley has subsequently been redeveloped with the large single-tiered East Stand and two-tiered North and West Stands; the Jimmy Seed Stand remains a small single-tiered structure.

Coventry City

Coventry City was founded in 1883 by workers at the Singer cycle factory. They moved to Highfield Road in 1899. In 1908 the club built a new stand with a roof on the Thackhall Street side. Further developments were made, including the erection of the Kop in 1922 and a cover over the West Terrace. A Main Stand was built to replace the original stand on the south side of the pitch. Two years later terracing was extended at the Kop's north corner, known as the Crow's Nest. Jimmy Hill's appointment as manager in 1961 brought in sweeping changes. The Thackhall Street Stand had seats added and the new Sky Blue Stand was built. With Hill as chairman Highfield Road became England's first all-seater stadium in 1981. During the 1990s the new all-seater East Stand (formerly the Kop) was built and the Main Stand re-roofed. The 2004-5 season was the club's last at Highfield Road and they have now moved to the Ricoh Arena.

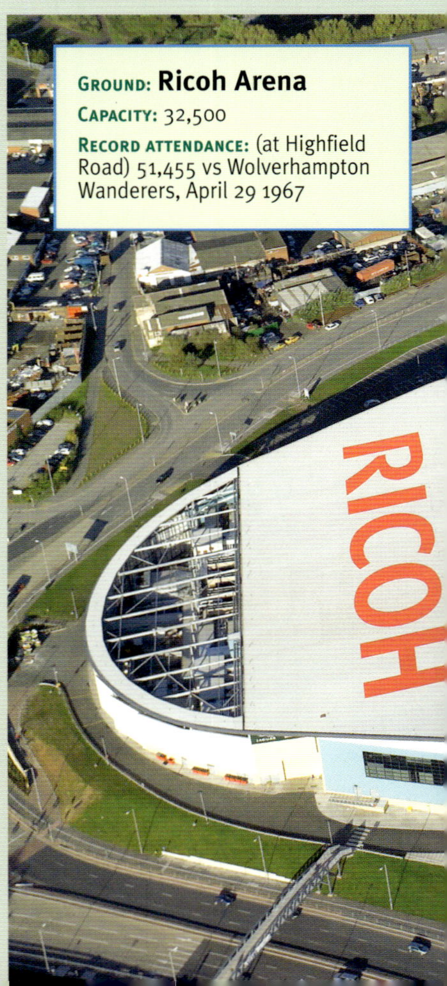

GROUND: Ricoh Arena

CAPACITY: 32,500

RECORD ATTENDANCE: (at Highfield Road) 51,455 vs Wolverhampton Wanderers, April 29 1967

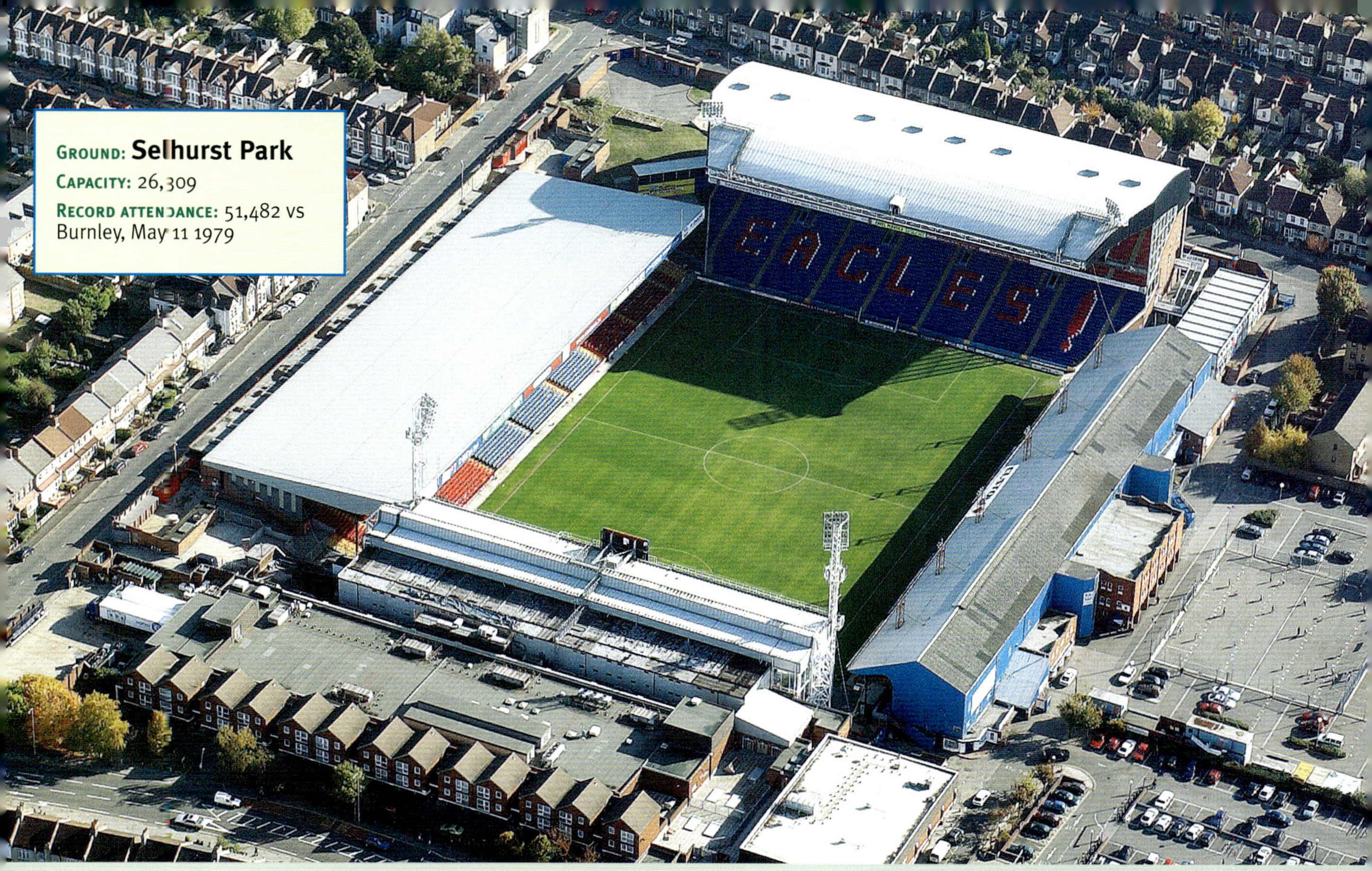

Ground: **Selhurst Park**
Capacity: 26,309
Record attendance: 51,482 vs Burnley, May 11 1979

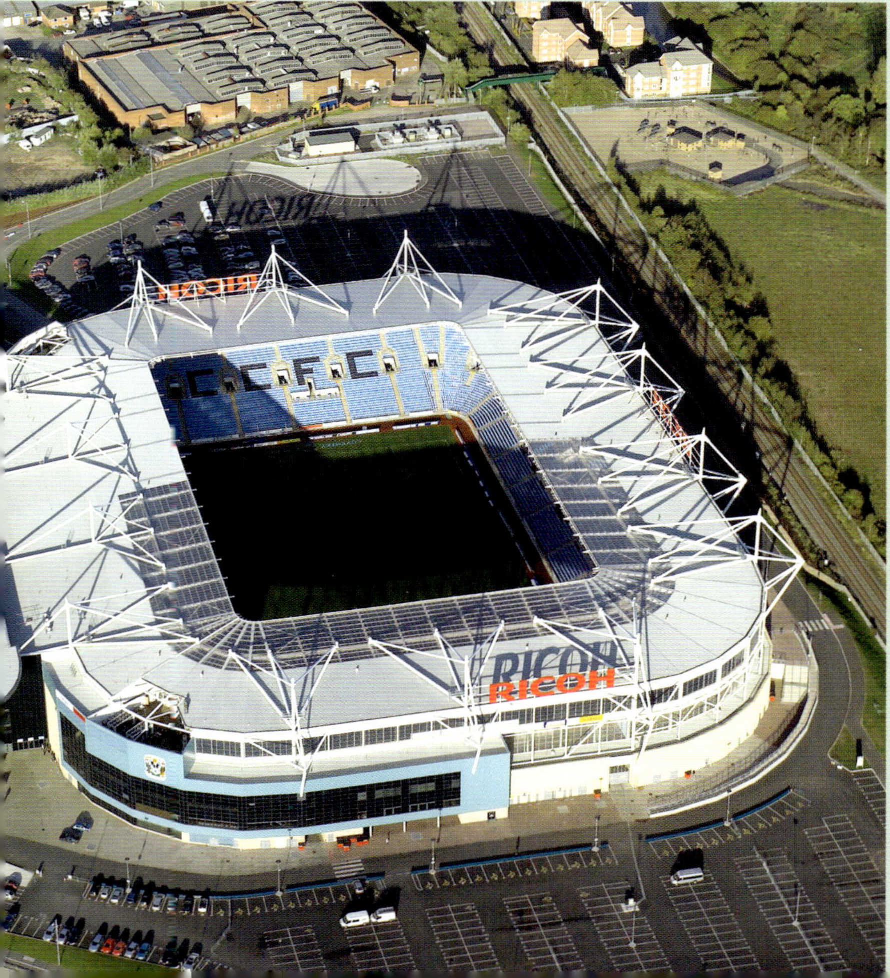

Crystal Palace was formed in 1905, when the club took up residence at the Crystal Palace Park ground, England's national stadium. In 1915 the team moved on to the Herne Hill cycle and athletics ground and in 1918 to the Nest, a ground situated opposite Selhurst station. In 1919 Crystal Palace paid £2,570 for a former brickfield, Selhurst Park. Plans for development were fairly modest, with one stand and minimal terracing. The Main Stand was built to a similar design to those at Chelsea and Fulham. In 1969 the uncovered Park Side was developed into a stand with a 42m deep roof covering the original banking. The 1980s saw the first ever long-term ground-sharing arrangement at Selhurst Park, firstly with local rivals Charlton Athletic and then with Wimbledon. In the 1990s the Arthur Wait Stand was converted to all-seater and the Whitehorse Lane Stand was developed. In 1995 the Holmesdale Road Stand opened. This massive structure, built into a natural embankment and surrounded by houses, took more than a year to build; it opened in August 1995.

Derby County was formed by players from Derby County Cricket Club in 1884. Their first pitch was part of the cricket ground, which was in the middle of a race-course. Derby soon tired of rescheduling games that clashed with race meetings, and in 1895 they moved to a baseball ground that owner Francis Ley had built after a visit to the US. The club bought the Baseball Ground from Francis Ley in 1924. A two-tiered stand, opened in 1933, was built where the Osmanton Terrace and Catcher's Corner had stood. By the start of WWII all four sides of the Baseball Ground had been rebuilt and covered. The Rams returned to the First Division in 1969 under the management of Brian Clough; this was the same year the Ley Stand opened. Crowd trouble in the late 1970s and 1980s saw fences and barriers erected. Robert Maxwell took over as chairman in 1984; the fences came down in 1989 and after the Taylor report the club rebuilt the stadium. In 1995 they moved to Pride Park. The £16m project took 46 weeks and the Rams moved in at the beginning of the 1997/98 season.

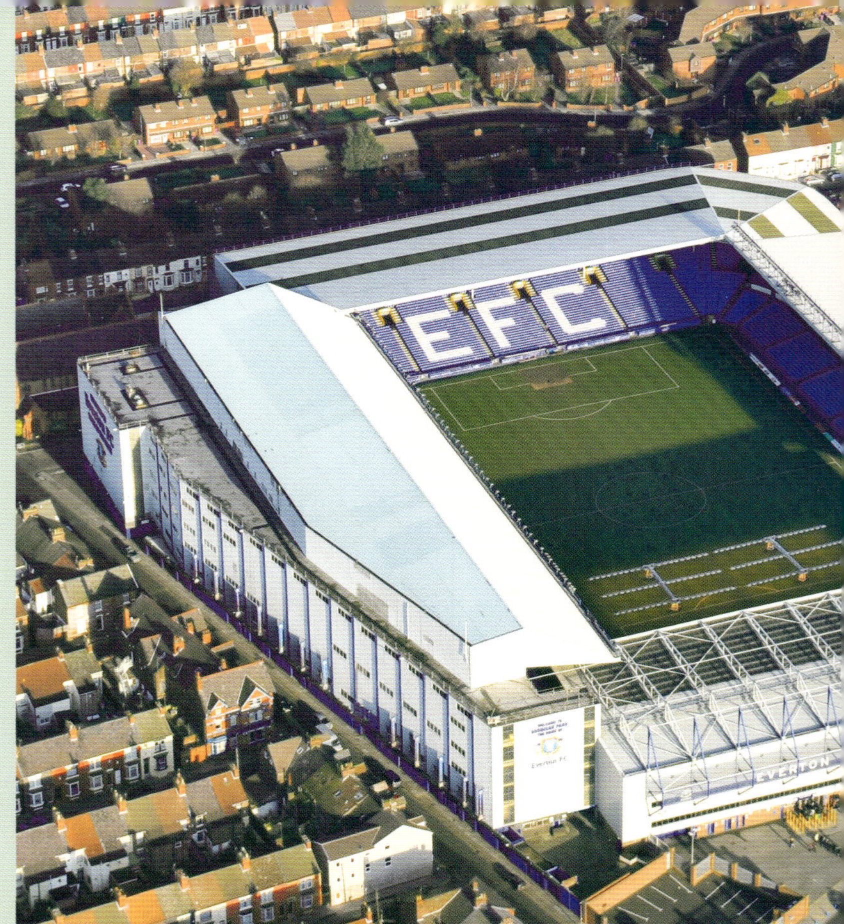

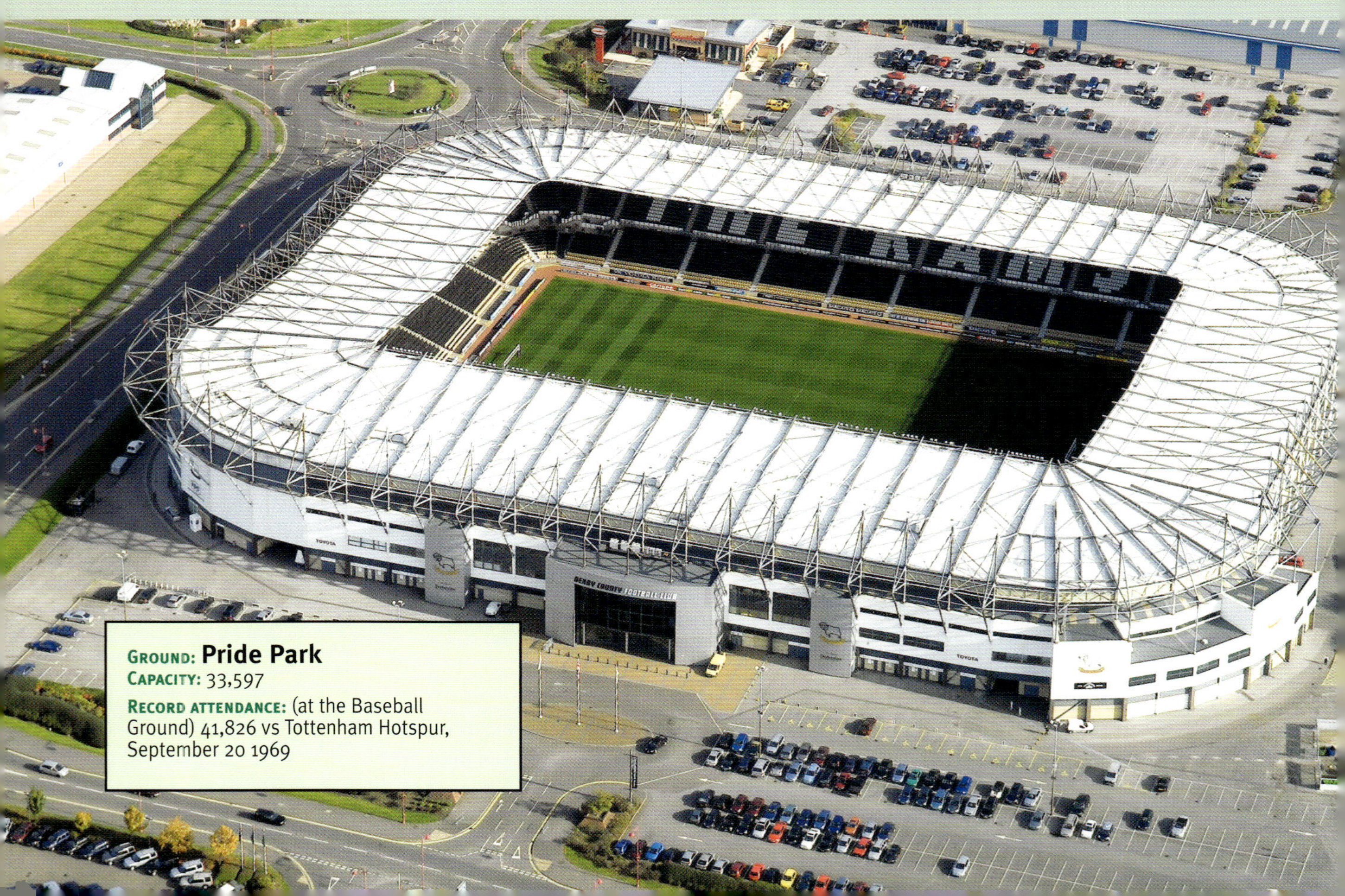

GROUND: **Pride Park**
CAPACITY: 33,597
RECORD ATTENDANCE: (at the Baseball Ground) 41,826 vs Tottenham Hotspur, September 20 1969

Fulham started in 1879 as Fulham St Andrews, a church team. The club moved grounds eight times before they finally arrived at Craven Cottage in 1896. The ground was on the site of the original Craven Cottage, built in 1789 by Baron Craven and burned down in 1888. They turned professional in 1898 and by 1905 were more successful than neighbouring Chelsea, drawing crowds in the region of 20,000. £15,000 was spent developing the ground; this included three terraces and a corner pavilion, the Cottage. The only stand to be built was on Stevenage Road, which had an upper tier of seats, a paddock in front covered by a pitched roof and gable in the centre. In 1961 the Hammersmith End was extended and in 1965 it was covered. The Riverside Terrace was replaced by the Riverside Stand in 1971, although the cost of this stand almost bankrupted the club. For the next 20 years Fulham declined. Their fortunes turned completely on May 29 1997 when Harrods' owner Mohammed Al Fayed bought the club. He had a five-year plan to get the club into the Premiership and in just four years this dream was realised. In 2002 Fulham left Craven Cottage to ground-share at QPR's Loftus Road. At the start of the 2004/05 season the Cottagers moved back to an improved Craven Cottage.

Ground: **Craven Cottage**
Capacity: 26,300
Record attendance: 49,335 vs Millwall, October 8 1938

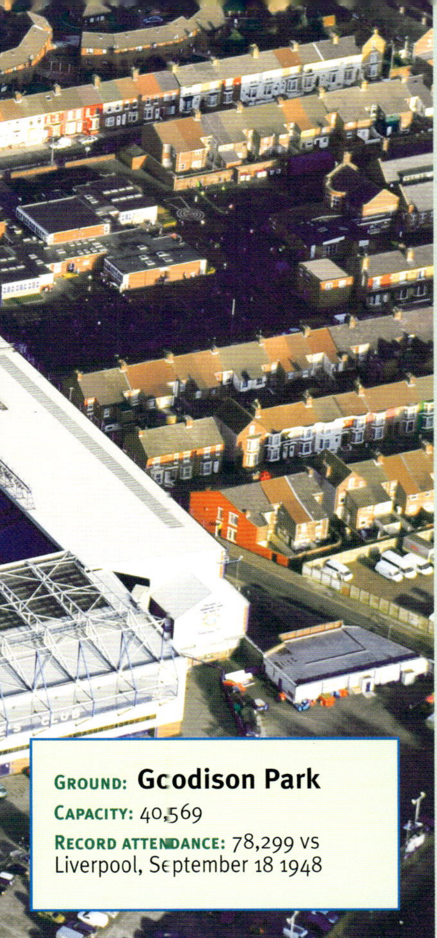

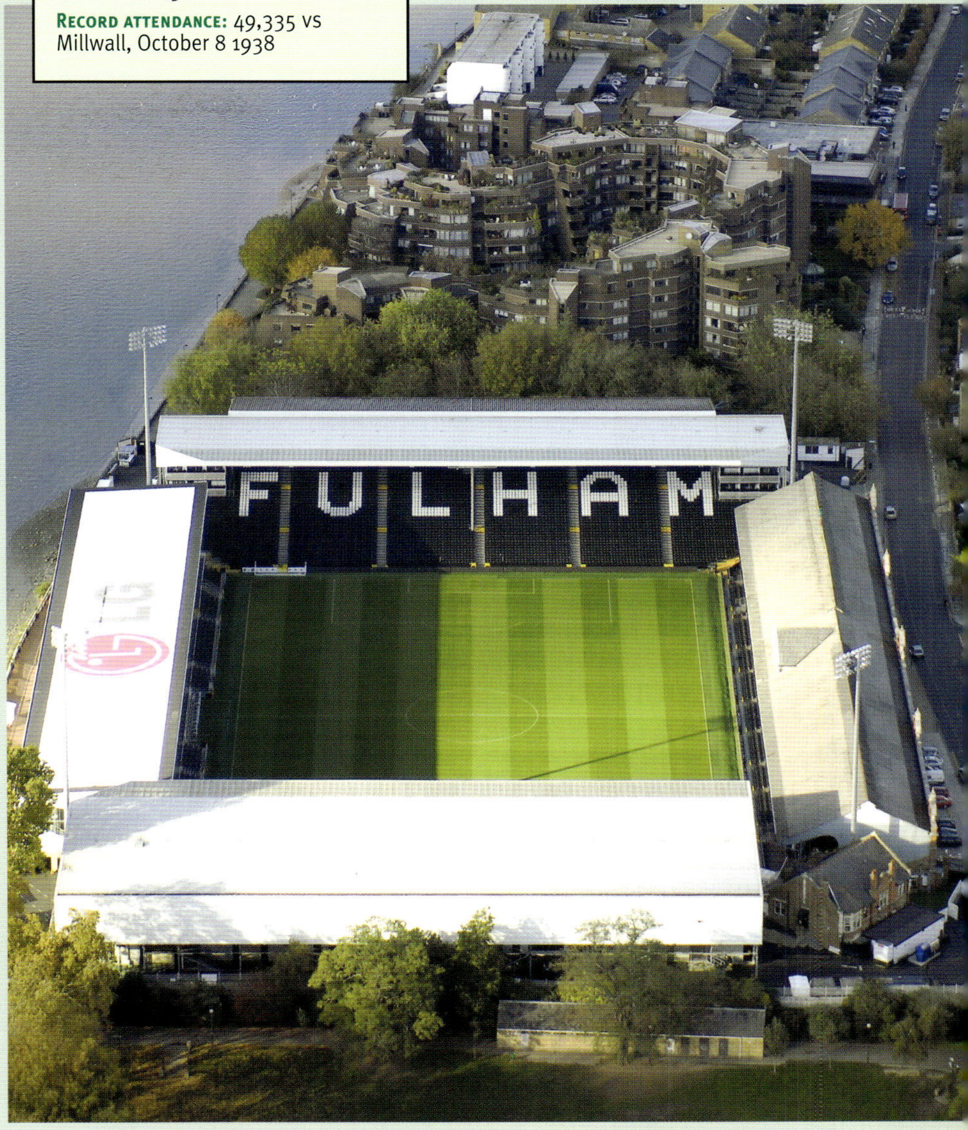

Ground: **Goodison Park**
Capacity: 40,569
Record attendance: 78,299 vs Liverpool, September 18 1948

Everton began as St Domingo's FC in 1878, playing games at Stanley Park. In 1884 the club became the first tenants at Anfield, and changed their name to Everton. In 1892 they moved to Goodison Park, then called Mere Green. They built two uncovered stands and a third covered stand with seating. Mere Green was renamed Goodison Park in 1892. The FA allowed the 1894 Cup Final to be played there. In 1895 the Bullens Road Stand was built. The Goodison Road Terrace was covered and by 1905 the ground had an estimated capacity of 55,000. In 1907 the two-tiered Park End Stand was built and in 1909 the magnificent Main Stand. In 1926 a two-tiered stand was built on the Bullens Road side. Twelve years later this was linked to the Gladwys Street end, making Goodison the first to have two-tiered stands on all sides. In the 1970s the new three-tier Main Stand was built. After the Taylor report, seats were added to the remaining terraces, and in 1994 the new single-tier Park End Stand was built.

Hampden Park is the home of Queen's Park, Scotland's oldest football club dating back to 1867. The club played its early games at Queen's Park Recreation Ground before moving to their own ground, the first Hampden Park on Queen's Drive, in 1873. They moved to Titwood Park in 1883 before moving again to the second Hampden Park in 1884. It was not long before the ground was also being used for Scottish FA Cup finals. The club moved once again in 1903 to a yet larger site, the third Hampden Park, which had a capacity of 65,000. Scottish architect Archibald Leitch designed the ground's two stands on the south side with a pavilion in between and an oval bowl of terracing around the rest of the ground. The club continued to do well, finishing fifth in the Scottish First Division in 1929. Further developments took place in the 1930s when the North Stand was built at the back of the Main Stand terracing, bringing the capacity up to 150,000. This led to the ground being used for international games and in 1937 the highest crowd ever to attend a football game – 149,415 fans – packed in to see Scotland play England. Until the 1950s Hampden Park was the largest ground in the world. In the 1960s a roof was added to the West Stand but the club lacked funds to carry out other refurbishments. During the 1970s Hampden Park's future hung in the balance as the Scottish FA tried to decide how the renovations would be funded. By 1981 an appeal had raised the necessary funds to begin redeveloping the ground. The North

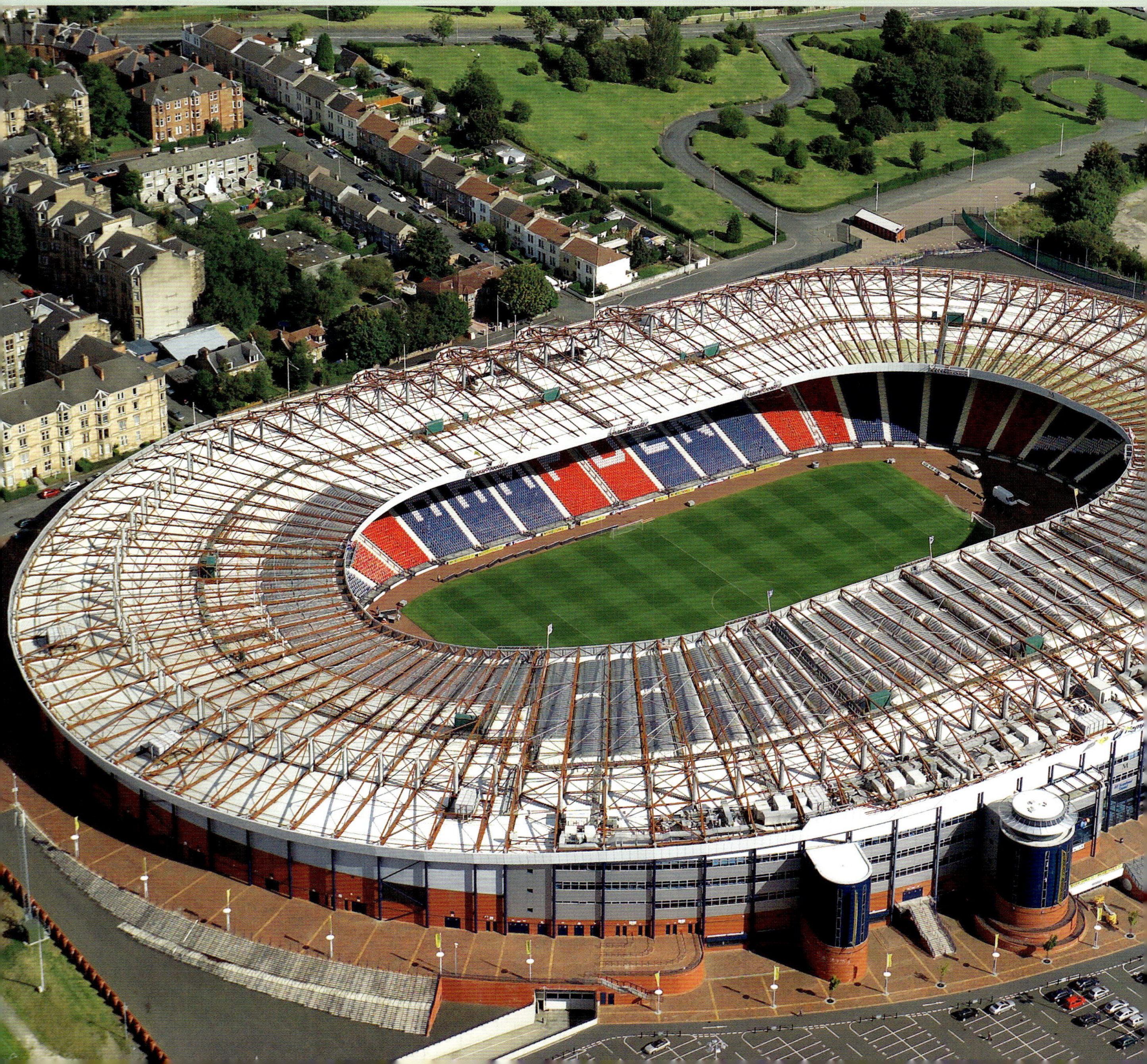

Stand was demolished. The next phase was delayed as the Taylor report requirements meant that proposed developments were costly. Some commentators even began to question whether it was cost-effective to renovate the ground since Ibrox and Murrayfield were close by. Eventually the decision was made to renovate the ground and in 1992 work began. Seats and roofs were added to the North and East Stands. Queen's Park remains the only amateur football club still in the Scottish Football League.

GROUND: Hampden Park
CAPACITY: 52,000
RECORD INTERNATIONAL ATTENDANCE: 149,415 vs England, April 17 1937, the all-time highest attendance in Europe
RECORD CLUB ATTENDANCE: 95,772 vs Rangers, January 12 1929

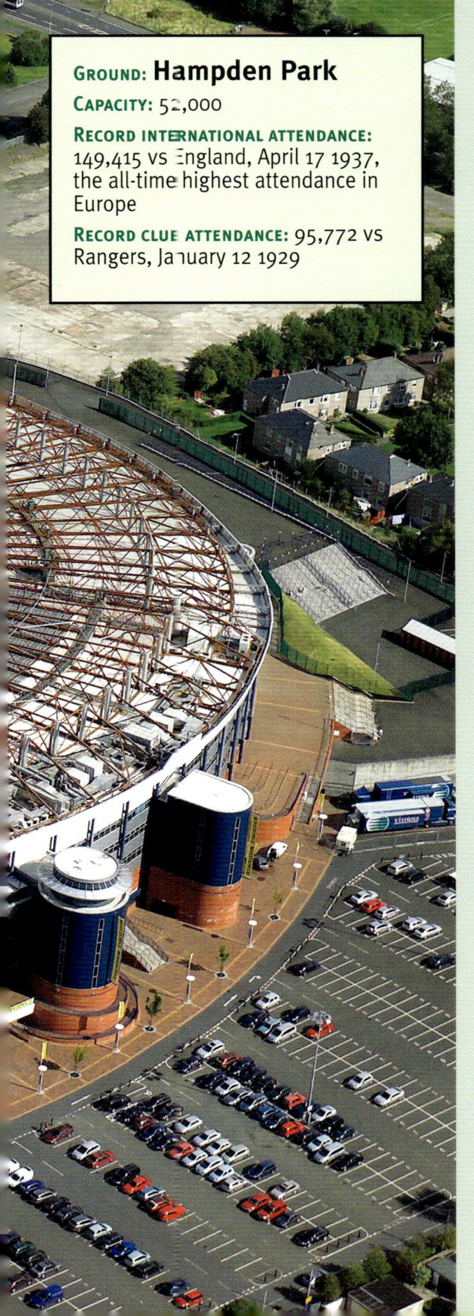

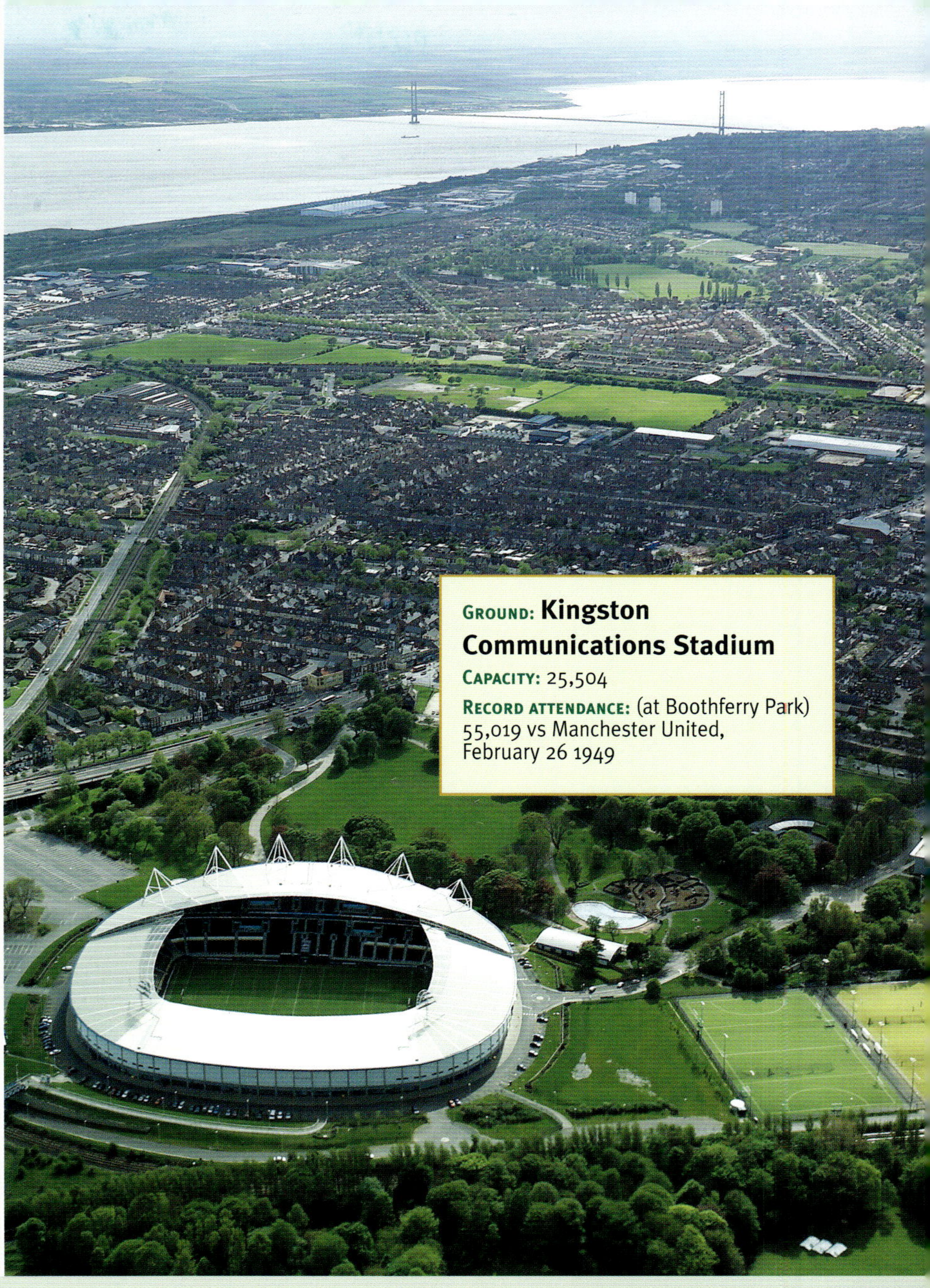

GROUND: Kingston Communications Stadium
CAPACITY: 25,504
RECORD ATTENDANCE: (at Boothferry Park) 55,019 vs Manchester United, February 26 1949

Hull City formed in 1904 and shared the Boulevard ground with Hull FC, a rugby league club. It was closed following crowd trouble at a rugby match and the Tigers moved to the Circle, home of Hull Cricket Club. The club laid out a pitch next to the cricket oval in 1906 and called it Anlaby Road. A main stand was erected in 1914 and covers added in the 1920s. The Tigers remained there until the Second World War, and re-formed in 1944, moving to Boothferry Park in 1946. The first stand was the 8,000-seater West Stand, followed by a cover over the North Stand. The North Stand was extended in 1950 and seats were added. Boothferry Park had its own railway station and the first train service began in 1951. The new South Stand was built in 1964 but City's fortunes slipped and they found themselves in Division Four by the 1980s. By 1982 the club went into receivership. The ground fell into a bad state of repair and the North Stand was sold off to a supermarket. In 2002 Hull moved back to the Circle, to the Kingston Communications Stadium, a £44m purpose-built ground. The structure is completely enclosed, with a large two-tiered west stand and single-tiered stands on the other three sides.

Ipswich Town

Ipswich Town began life as Ipswich AFC in 1878. The club's first ground was on Broom Hill. In 1888 the football team merged with the rugby team to become Ipswich Town and moved to Portman Road. The rugby team broke away in 1893 but Town continued to share with East Suffolk Cricket Club. There was a wooden stand along the Portman Road side but nothing else divided the two pitches. Town turned professional in 1936. In 1937 more terracing and seats were added. In 1957, under Alf Ramsey, Ipswich was promoted to Division Two and constructed the West Stand. The next major changes took place in the 1980s when the West Stand was extended and renamed the Pioneer Stand. Portman Road became the first Premier League ground to become all-seater. The developments continued and the Greene King, or South Stand, opened in 2001 and a year later the new North Stand was opened.

Leeds United

Leeds United started life in 1904 as Leeds City FC. Their ground Elland Road was originally a grass field, known as the Old Peacock ground, named after the pub which stood opposite. Leeds City bought the ground from Holbeck Rugby Club and in 1905 they built the West Stand. Leeds United re-formed in 1920 from the remnants of Leeds City, which was disbanded after the club was accused of making illegal payments to players. During the 1920s, ground development continued with the erection of the terraces popularly known as the Scratching Shed and the Spion Kop. In the 1960s the success of the team brought in money to fund the building of the new Kop in 1968, when Leeds first became First Division champions. In 1974 the Scratching Shed was replaced by the South Stand. The East Stand was completed in 1992-3. Now Elland Road boasts the world's largest cantilevered stand.

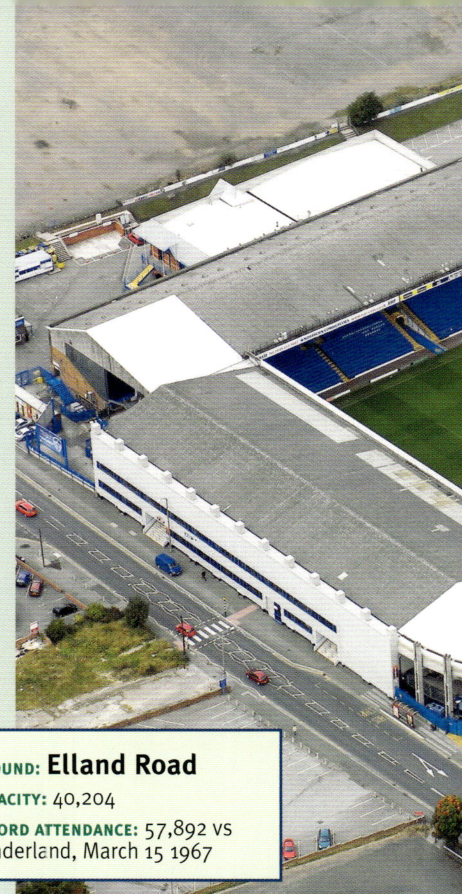

GROUND: Elland Road
CAPACITY: 40,204
RECORD ATTENDANCE: 57,892 vs Sunderland, March 15 1967

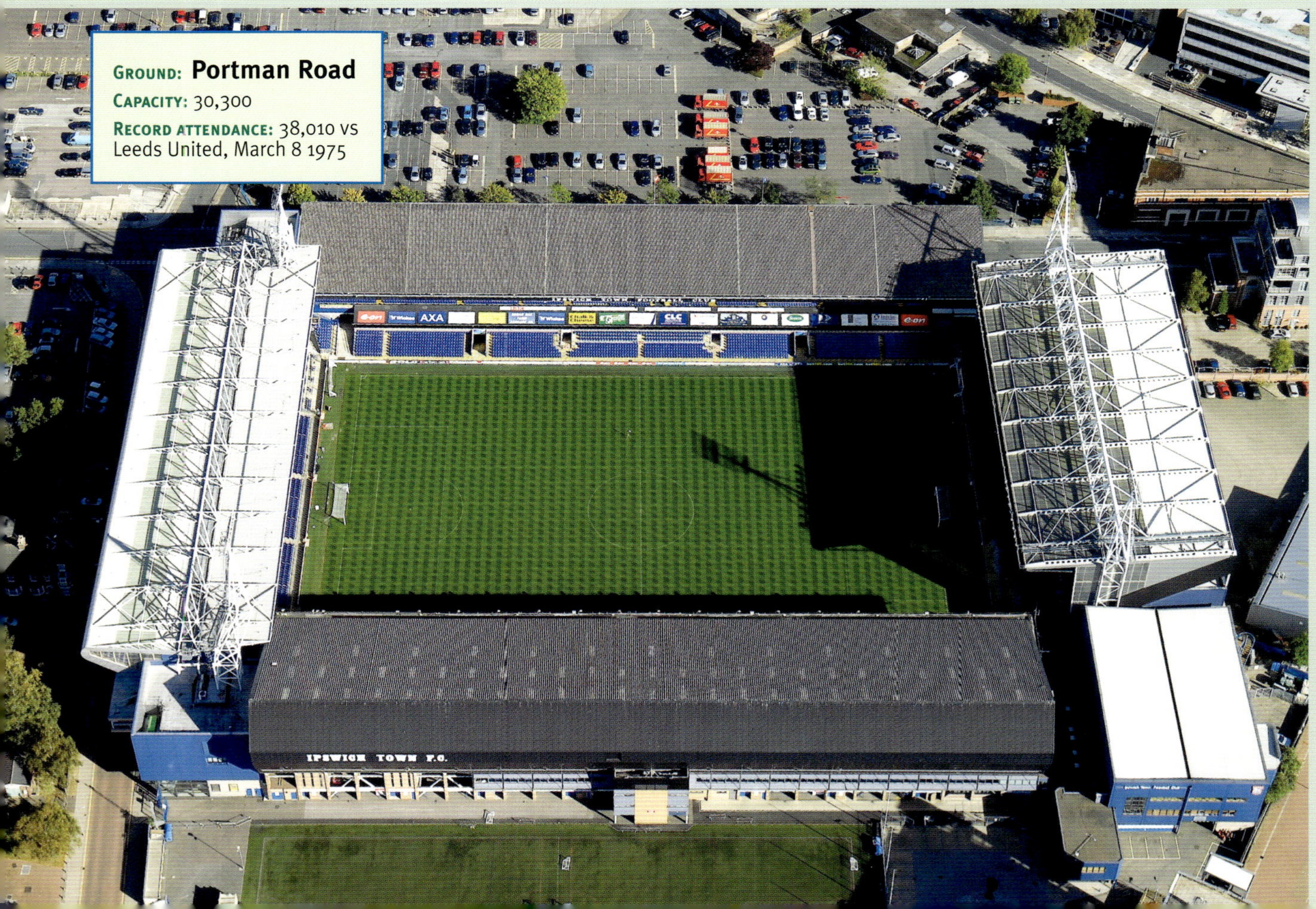

GROUND: Portman Road
CAPACITY: 30,300
RECORD ATTENDANCE: 38,010 vs Leeds United, March 8 1975

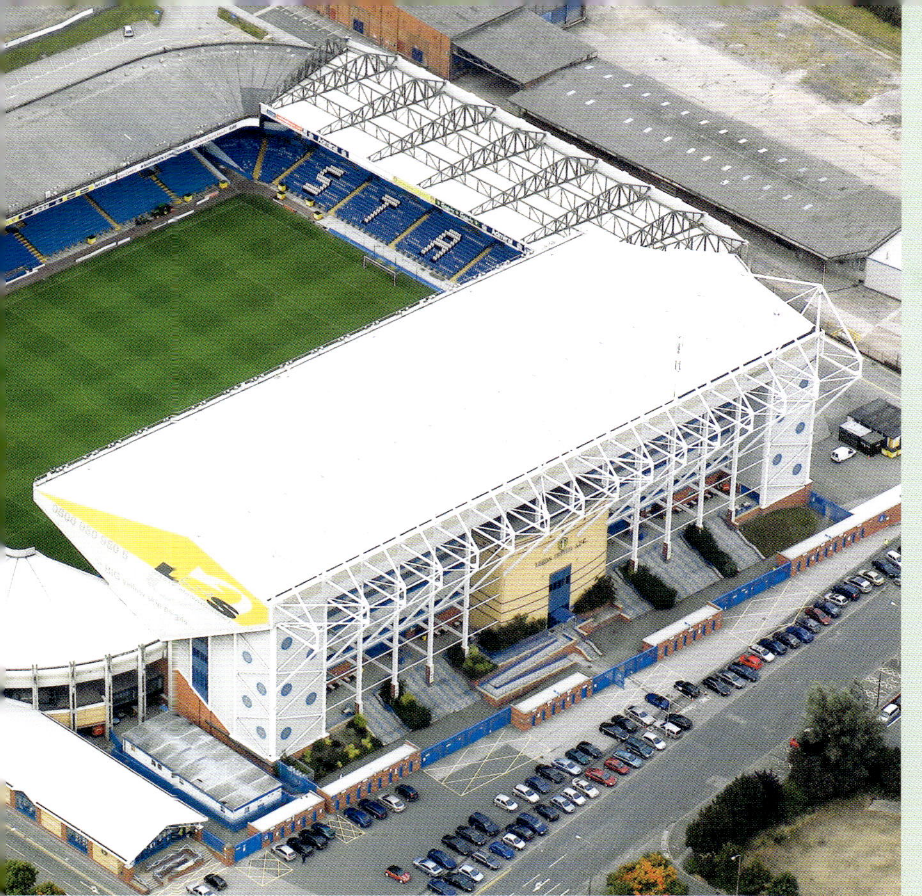

Leicester City

Leicester City was established in 1884 as Leicester Fosse. In their first year the team played at the racecourse before moving the following year to Victoria Park. In 1889 the club turned professional and moved to Mill Lane, which they left two years later when they moved to Filbert Street. The ground was then known as Walnut Street and the facilities included a low main stand. Major developments began after WWI when they changed their name to Leicester City. In 1921 the new Main Stand was opened. In 1927 the club built a two-tier stand at the Kop End and moved the Kop to the Filbert Street End. In 1971 the Filbert Street Terrace became the North Stand and the Popular Side was turned into the all-seater East Stand. In the 1990s the club rebuilt the Main Stand. However, the ground was still cramped and in 2002 the club moved to the Walkers Stadium, a short distance from the Filbert Street ground.

GROUND: **Walkers Stadium**

CAPACITY: 32,500

RECORD ATTENDANCE: (at Filbert Street) 47,298 vs Tottenham Hotspur, February 18 1928

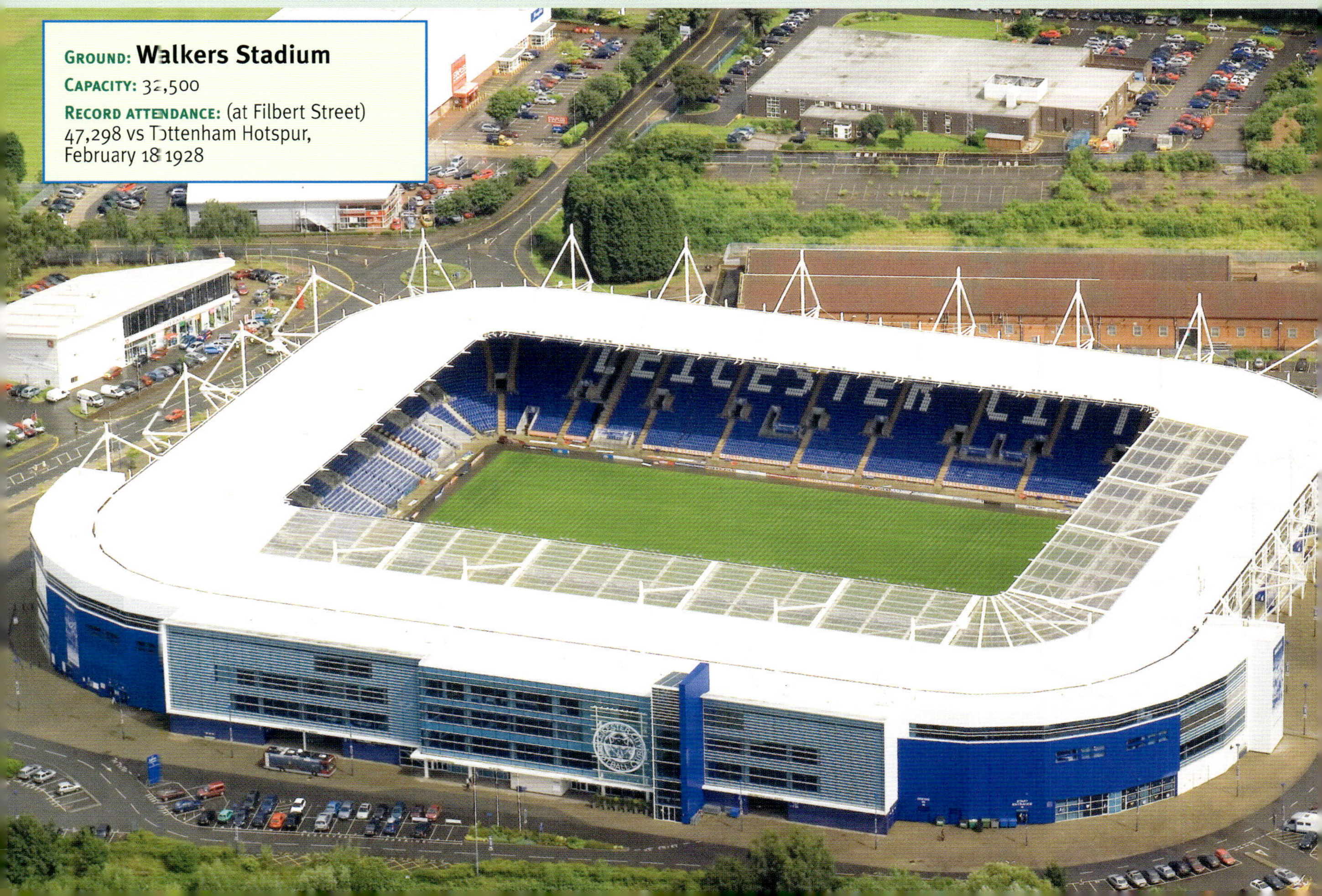

Liverpool Anfield was originally home to Everton, who played there from 1884 until 1892, when they had a disagreement with Anfield's owner John Houlding and moved to Goodison Park. Houlding set up his own team, Liverpool, dominated by Scottish players. Major changes took place at Anfield in 1906, the season Liverpool won their second League title. The pitch was raised by five feet and, in addition to the two sides which were already covered, a new main stand and south terrace, the Kop, were built. The Kop was one of the tallest terraces in England, complete with a 50ft flagpole, and was covered in 1928, when it became Britain's largest covered terrace, with a capacity of 28,000. The Kemlyn Road Stand was rebuilt and reopened in 1964, the same season that Liverpool won their first FA Cup final. The 1970s saw the Main Stand extended, and the club began buying houses along Kemlyn Road so they could build a second tier on the Kemlyn Road Stand. It was not until 1990 that the final tenants – two elderly sisters – agreed to sell up. On April 15 1989 96 Liverpool fans were crushed to death at Hillsborough in Sheffield. The resulting Taylor report had a massive impact on football grounds across the country. At Anfield plans were drawn up to make the Kop all-seater, so that a tragedy on the scale of Hillsborough could never happen again. In 1994 the Kop was finally demolished.

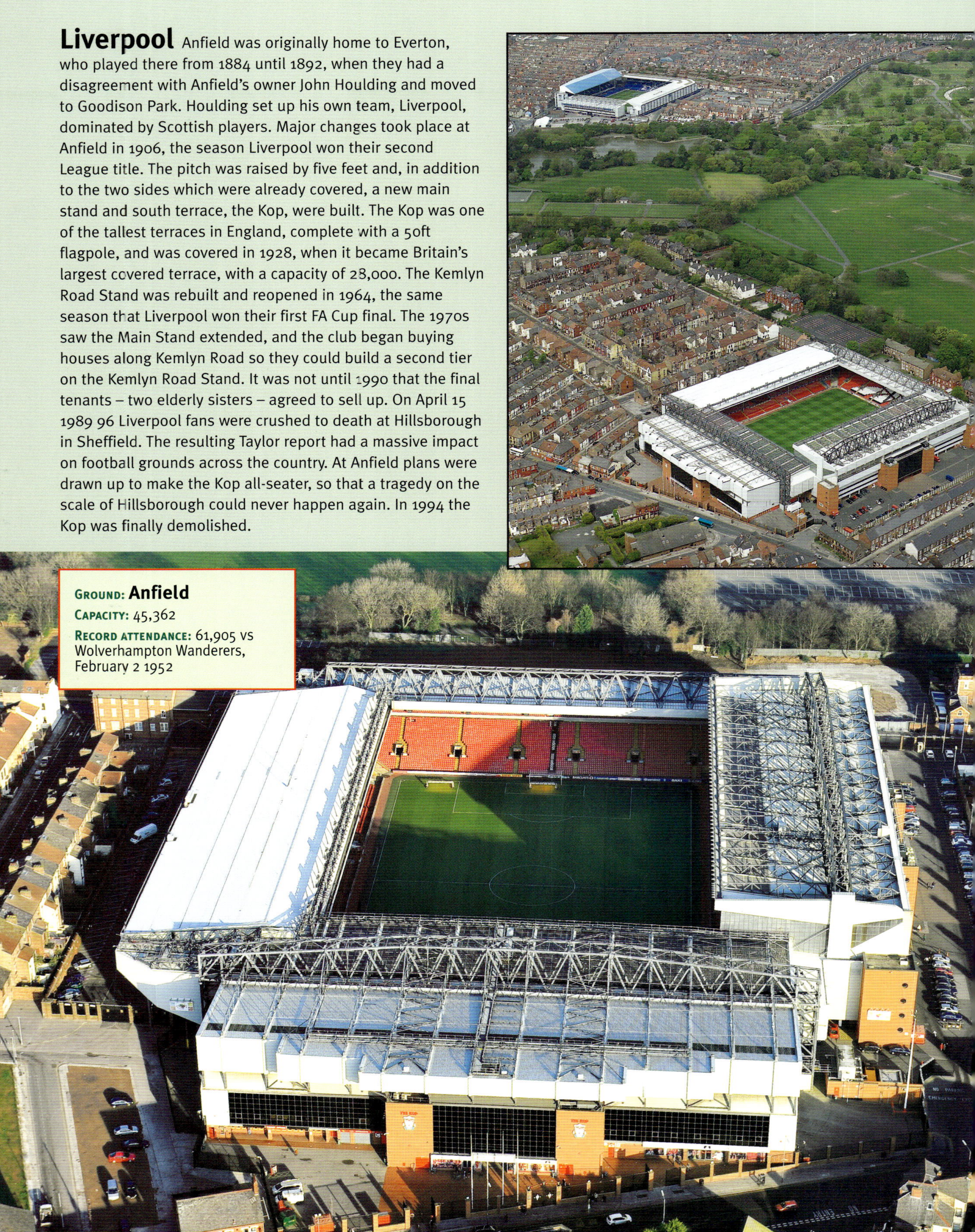

GROUND: Anfield
CAPACITY: 45,362
RECORD ATTENDANCE: 61,905 vs Wolverhampton Wanderers, February 2 1952

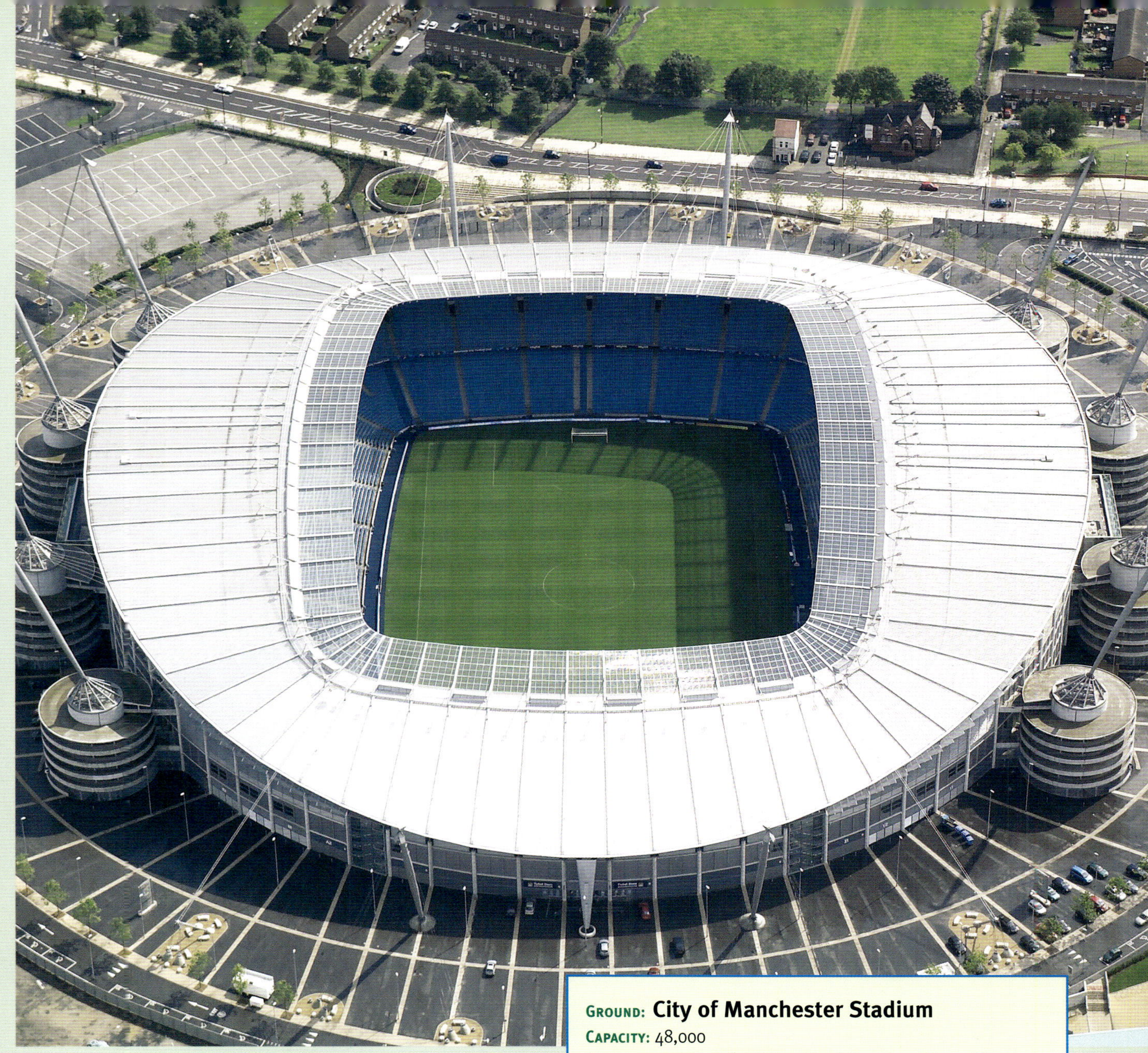

Ground: City of Manchester Stadium
Capacity: 48,000
Record attendance: (at Maine Road) 84,569 vs Stoke City, March 3 1934

Manchester City began life as an amalgamation between West Gorton and Gorton Athletic in 1887. At first the club played as Ardwick before changing their name to Manchester City in 1894. The team initially played games on Hyde Road, a small ground penned in by a railway line and houses, which had two stands, paid for with the help of a local brewery. In 1920, the Main Stand burned down and the club decided it was time to move. At the start of the 1923 season they opened the doors to their new home at Maine Road. The ground was vast: in the 1920s it had a capacity in excess of 80,000 and regular gates of 37,000, the highest gates in the League. Following the Second World War, local rivals Manchester United became lodgers at Maine Road and profits soared. The Blues spent some of this money on wooden benches, which were installed under the Platt Lane roof in the 1950s. In 1956 City won their third FA Cup and built a roof over the Kippax Terrace, leaving just the Scoreboard End uncovered. This end was replaced by the North Stand in 1971. Following the Taylor report, the Platt Lane Stand was demolished in 1992 and replaced by the Umbro Stand, which cost City £5m and plunged the club into debt. The report's requirements meant the club had to demolish the Kippax Terrace and replace it with an all-seater stand. The new stand cost £11m and brought Maine Road's capacity up to 32,344. Despite spending £19m on developments, the club left Maine Road in 2003 and became tenants of the brand new City of Manchester Stadium, built for the 2002 Commonwealth Games. The club spent £20m turning the athletics stadium into a football ground. The stadium is totally enclosed by two three-tiered stands and two two-tiered stands.

Manchester United dates from 1878 when it was formed by workers from the Lancashire and Yorkshire Railway. It was known as Newton Heath FC. The Heathens played early matches on North Road, before moving to Bank Street, Clayton in 1893, a year after joining the League. By 1902 their debts had grown so large they went into liquidation. Local brewer John H Davies rescued the club and changed the name to Manchester United. The club's fortunes on the pitch also changed; by 1906 they were back in the First Division and had cover on all sides of the ground, a main stand with a gallery and a total capacity of 50,000. In 1908, United won their first League title and in 1909 the FA Cup. A year later the club said farewell to Bank Street and moved five miles away to a new ground at Old Trafford. By then Davies had invested £60,000 and had developed the ground into a rectangle with curved corners and a multi-span Main Stand. In 1931 United were relegated, crowds dropped to 3,500 and the club faced bankruptcy. Up stepped James Gibson, a wealthy businessman, who cleared the club's debts and funded a cover over the United Road side. The ground was badly damaged during the war, and United began ground-sharing with Manchester City. It was not until 1949 that Old Trafford was refurbished and United returned. The pitched roof covering the south-west corner was expanded to cover the Stretford End in 1959, the year after the Munich air crash. The 1960s saw further developments at the ground, when Old Trafford was selected as a venue for World Cup games. In 1965 the club built a new two-tiered stand over the United Road Terrace capable of seating 10,000 and holding a further 10,000 standing. This new stand also held the first executive boxes at a European football ground. From then until the 1990s United gradually converted Old Trafford into a fully enclosed all-seater stadium. New plans to expand capacity were drawn up in 1995. The three-tiered North Stand opened in 1996 and second tiers were added to the East and West Stands in 2001. In 2006 north-east and north-west quadrants were opened bringing the capacity to 76,100, the largest League ground in Britain.

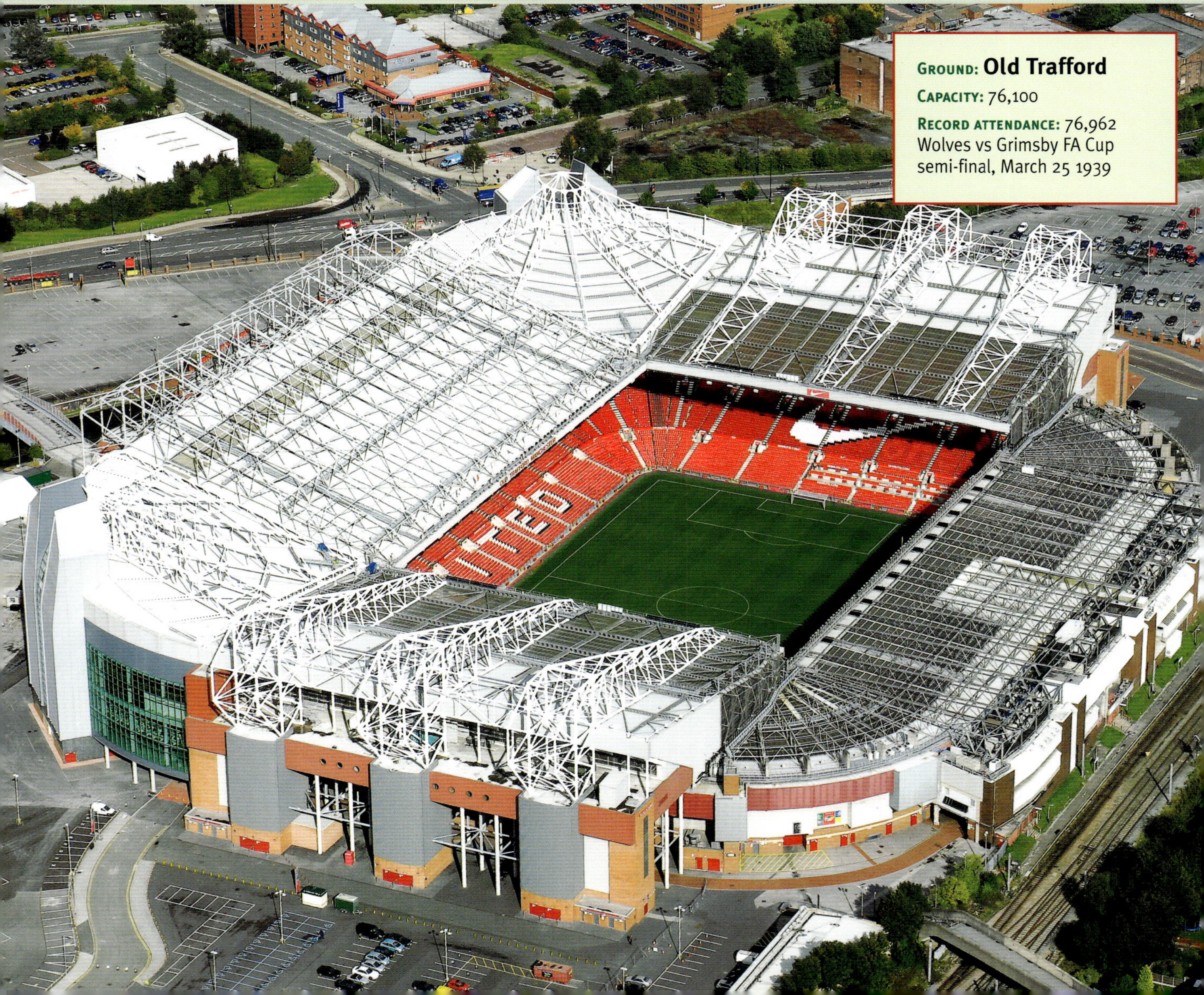

Ground: Old Trafford
Capacity: 76,100
Record attendance: 76,962
Wolves vs Grimsby FA Cup semi-final, March 25 1939

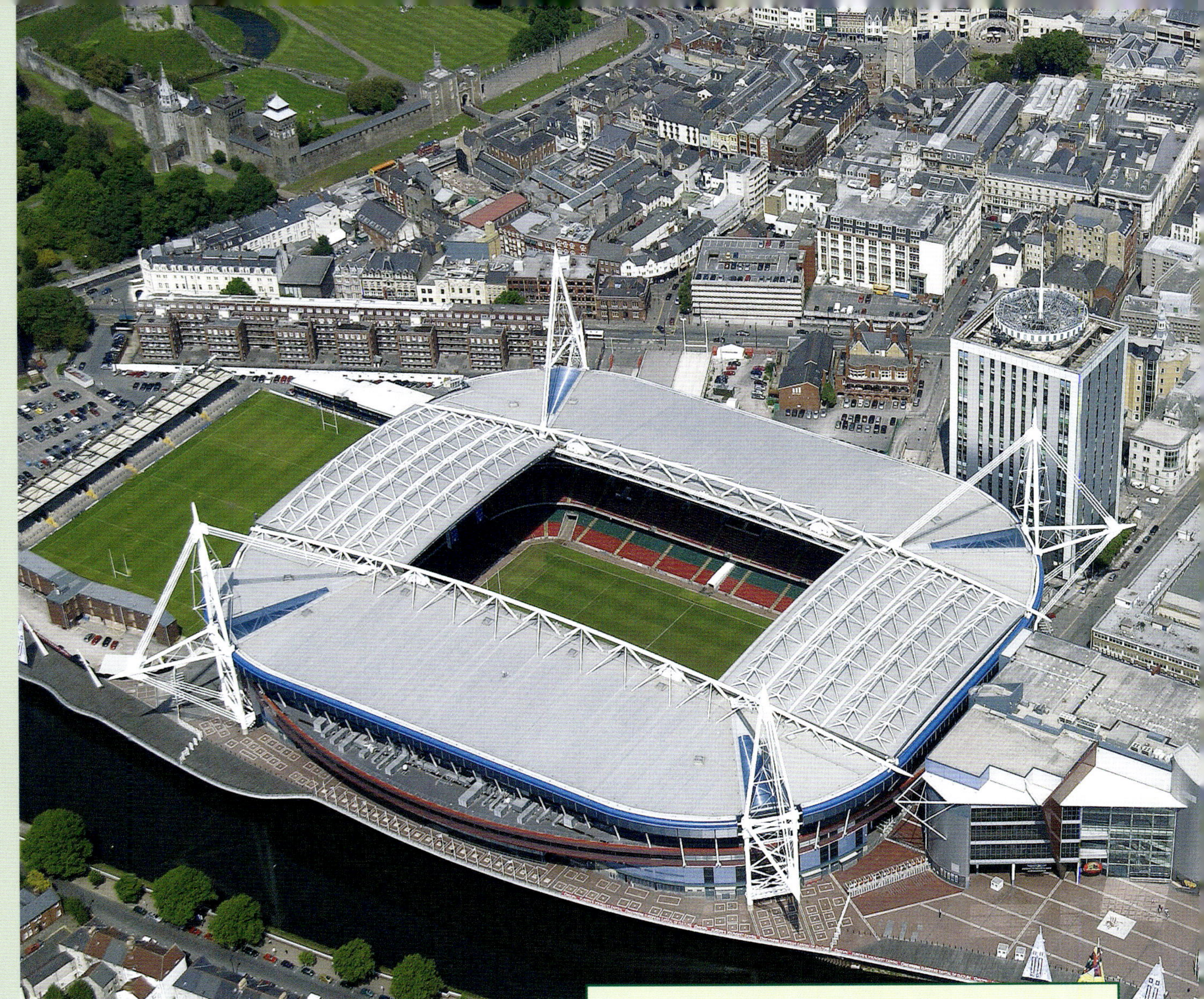

Ground: Millennium Stadium
Capacity: 74,500

The Millennium Stadium opened in October 1999 on the site of Cardiff Arms Park. The ground dates back to the 17th century but was not called Cardiff Arms Park until 1787. Cricket was the first sport played at the ground from 1848; rugby was played there from 1876. The Grandstand was opened in 1885, a year before football was first played there. An extension to the Grandstand was added in 1890, and a grand pavilion was built in 1904. The Grandstand was replaced by the South Stand in 1912. The Park's owner, Lord Bute, sold the ground in 1922 and the rugby and cricket clubs set up a joint company to take it over. The North Stand opened in 1934 and the South Stand was rebuilt in 1956 after Cardiff was selected to stage the 1958 Commonwealth Games. In 1968, the Welsh Rugby Union (WRU) took over Cardiff Arms Park and there followed a 16-year period of redevelopment. A new two-tiered stand was erected in place of the North Stand. The East Terrace opened in 1980 and the South Stand opened in 1984. Football returned to Cardiff Arms Park in 1989. Just six years later the WRU decided that the ground's 53,500 capacity was insufficient and submitted plans to the Millennium Commission for an ambitious 75,000-seater stadium to be created on the site of the Park. The Commission stumped up £50m and the other £114m was funded by commercial sources. The ground was built in time for the 1999 Rugby World Cup and quickly established itself as a unique sporting venue. The ground is home to Britain's first retractable roof and the grass is grown outside the ground and brought in when needed. It is completely enclosed with curved corners and three tiers on three sides. The North Stand remains a two-tier structure as it backs onto a rugby club, leaving no room for a third tier. Capacity is now 74,500; as well as rugby, the stadium stages football play-off finals, British Speedway Grand Prix races and concerts. During the construction of the new Wembley Stadium it was also used for FA Cup finals; the last one was the 2006 match between Liverpool and West Ham United.

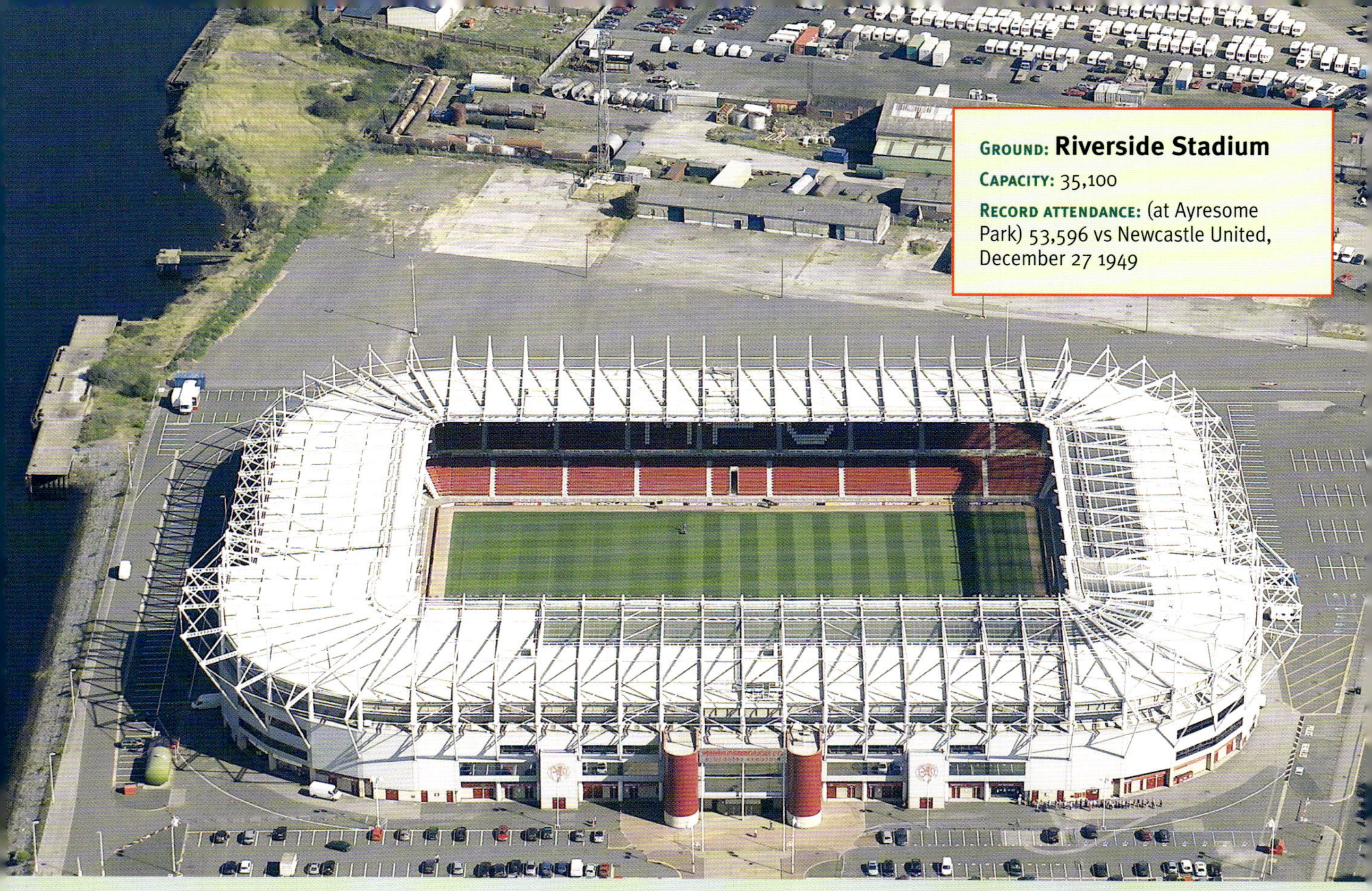

Ground: Riverside Stadium

Capacity: 35,100

Record attendance: (at Ayresome Park) 53,596 vs Newcastle United, December 27 1949

Middlesbrough

Middlesbrough was founded in 1876, but did not find a home until 1879, when the club moved first to Breckon Hill Road and a year later to Middlesbrough Cricket Club, Linthorpe Road. At Linthorpe Road they built a small stand and in 1899 joined the League. In 1903 they moved to Ayresome Park. Scottish architect Archibald Leitch built a stadium in nine months. It had a two-tier stand with a semi-circular gable and barrel roof, capable of seating 2,000, and incorporated the old stand from Linthorpe Road. In the 1930s the South Stand was replaced by a two-tier stand and the West End given a roof. Ayresome Park was a venue for some 1966 World Cup matches. In 1986 safety checks forced closure and the club played home games at Hartlepool. Following the Taylor report, £800,000 was spent on ground improvements: fences were removed, seats were installed in the South and East Stands and plans made for developing the North Stand. In 1994 Steve Gibson took a share in the club and in April 1995 Boro moved to the Riverside Stadium.

Newcastle United

Newcastle United began life as East End FC. The club formed in 1881 and first played at Chillingham Road in Heaton; they moved to St James' Park in 1892. Following the club's promotion in 1898, the ground's capacity of 15,000 was stretched. Terracing was cut into banks at the Leazes Park End and Leazes Terrace. In 1905, the wooden stands were cleared and three sides of banking were expanded. The West Stand was built with seating for 4,680. The ground opened in November 1905 with a capacity of 65,000. The 1920s saw more improvements. In 1971 the club was granted a 99-year lease on the ground and given permission to build a new 3,400-seater stand. In 1987 the 6,607-seater Jackie Milburn Stand was built. Sir John Hall joined the board in 1992 and took full control in 1994. He spent £23.5m on completely redeveloping St James' Park, with all-seater stands at each end and corner and additional tiers on the north and west sides and the north-west corner.

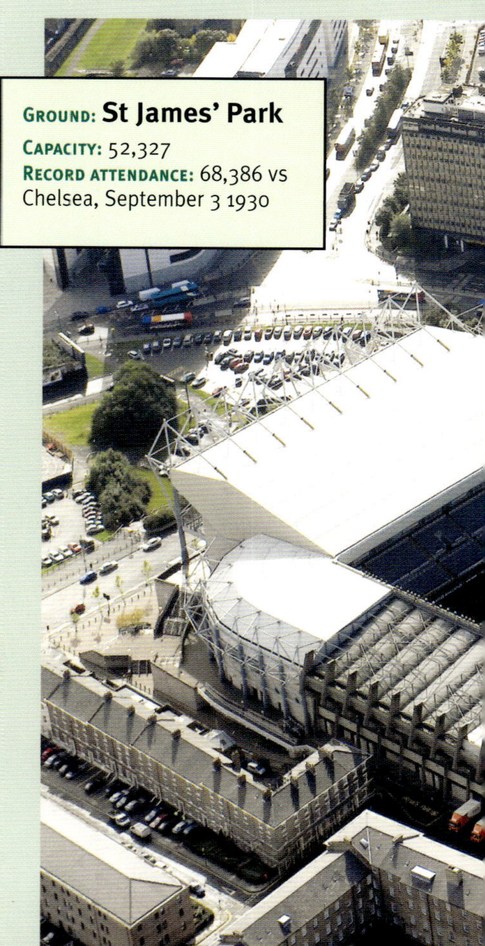

Ground: St James' Park

Capacity: 52,327

Record attendance: 68,386 vs Chelsea, September 3 1930

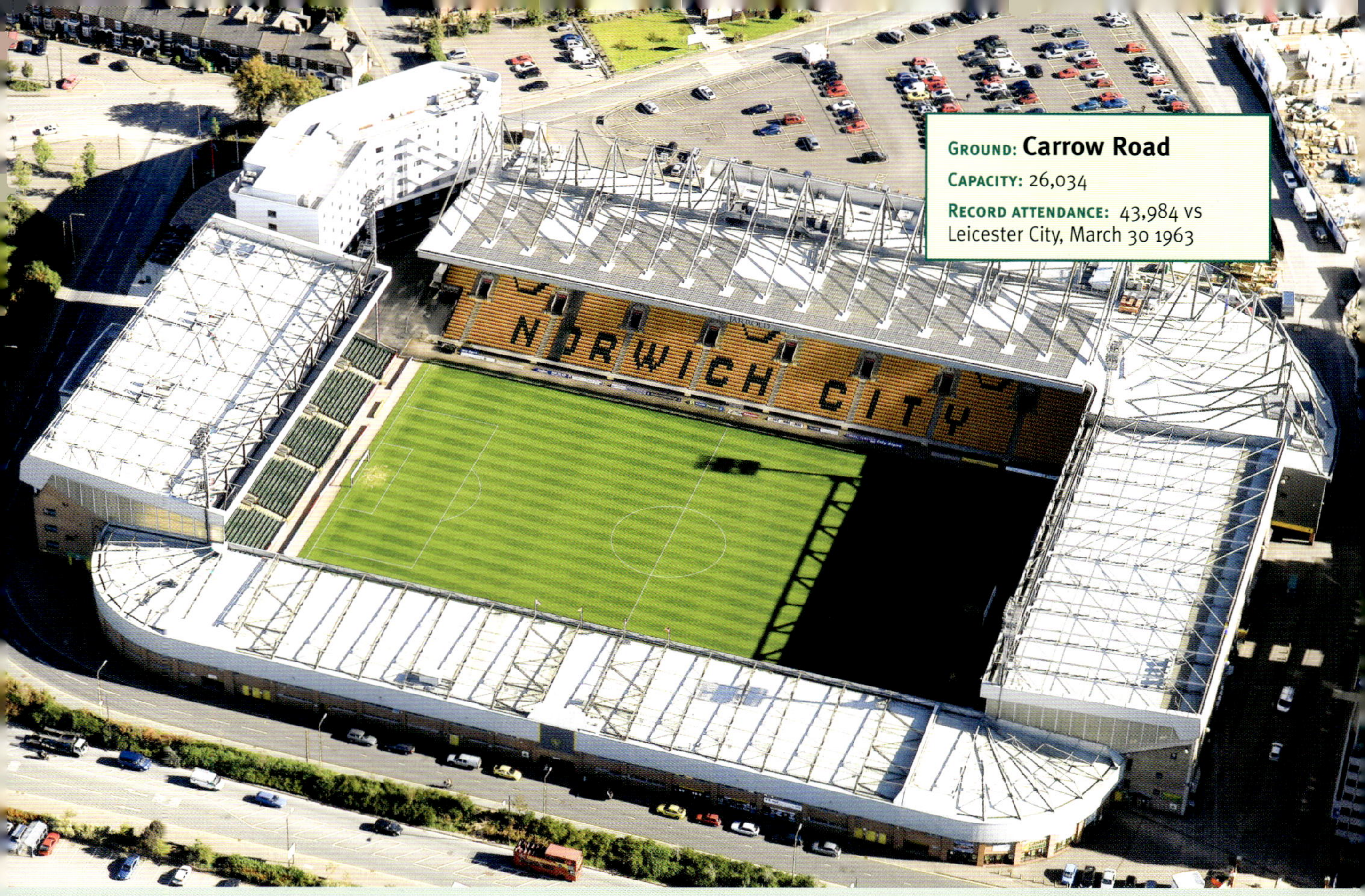

Ground: Carrow Road

Capacity: 26,034

Record attendance: 43,984 vs Leicester City, March 30 1963

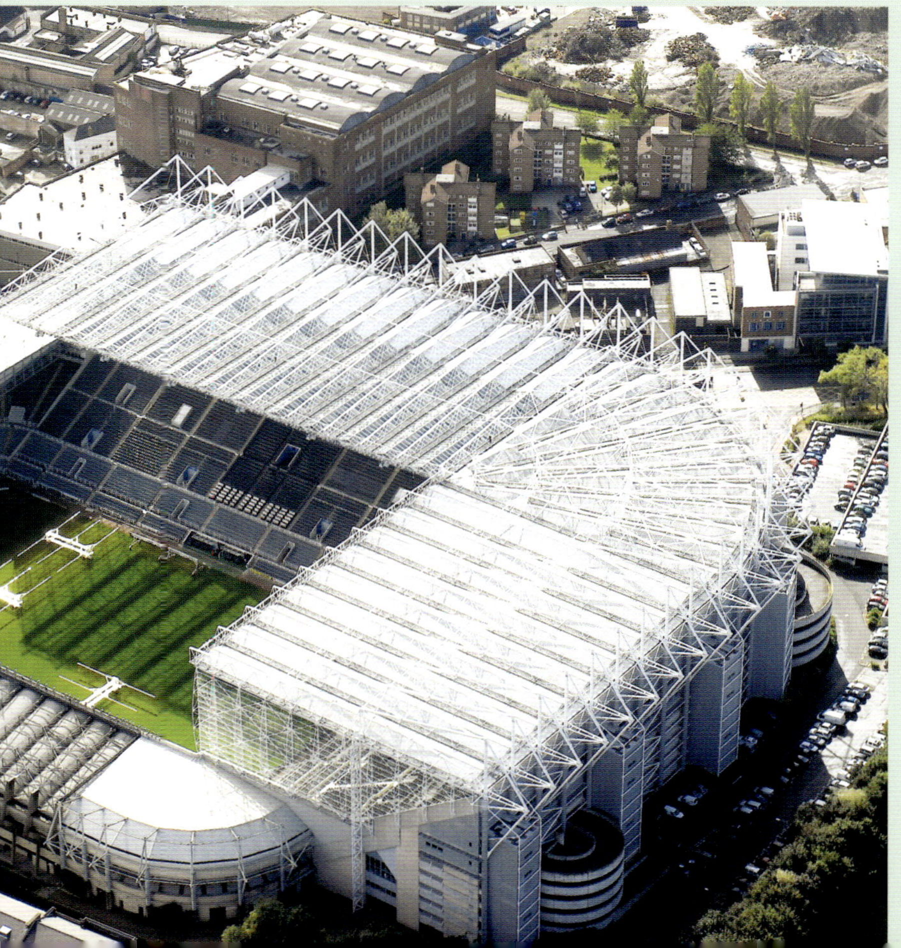

▲**Norwich City** formed in 1902 and their first ground on Newmarket Road belonged to the Norfolk County FA. The Canaries turned professional in 1905 and in 1908 moved to a new ground at Rosary Road called the Nest. In 1922 barriers collapsed and a boy was badly injured. Despite this, the club continued to play on the ground until 1935. That year the club moved to Carrow Road, a sports ground owned by Colman's Mustard. In just 82 days a 3,500-seater main stand was built. In 1937 the first terrace cover went up at the Station End, renamed the Barclay End. The terrace opposite the Main Stand was covered and in 1963 the South Stand was built. Fire destroyed the central section of the Main Stand in October 1984, which was replaced the following season. In the 1990s the ground was virtually rebuilt. New stands include the 8,000-seater Jarrold Road South Stand, opened in 2004. There are two-tiered stands at either end; the Geoffrey Watling City Stand is a smaller single-tiered stand.

Portsmouth formed in 1898. The club bought land near Fratton railway station and Fratton Park was opened in September 1899. A mock-Tudor pavilion complete with clock tower was built at the Frogmore Road entrance. In 1920 the club joined the League and were soon promoted to Division Two. In 1925 they opened the South Stand, which had 4,000 seats, a paddock and a balcony. In 1935 the club funded the building of the North Stand. By 1950 Pompey were drawing average gates of 39,000. The Fratton End was covered in 1956. Jim Gregory bought the club and between 1988-94 funded a £4m refurbishment programme. The Fratton End was demolished in 1988. In 1995 the ground was partly rebuilt and made all-seater bringing the capacity up to 20,288. Following the club's successful promotion to the Premiership in 2003, there are now plans to build a new stadium at the city's dockyard.

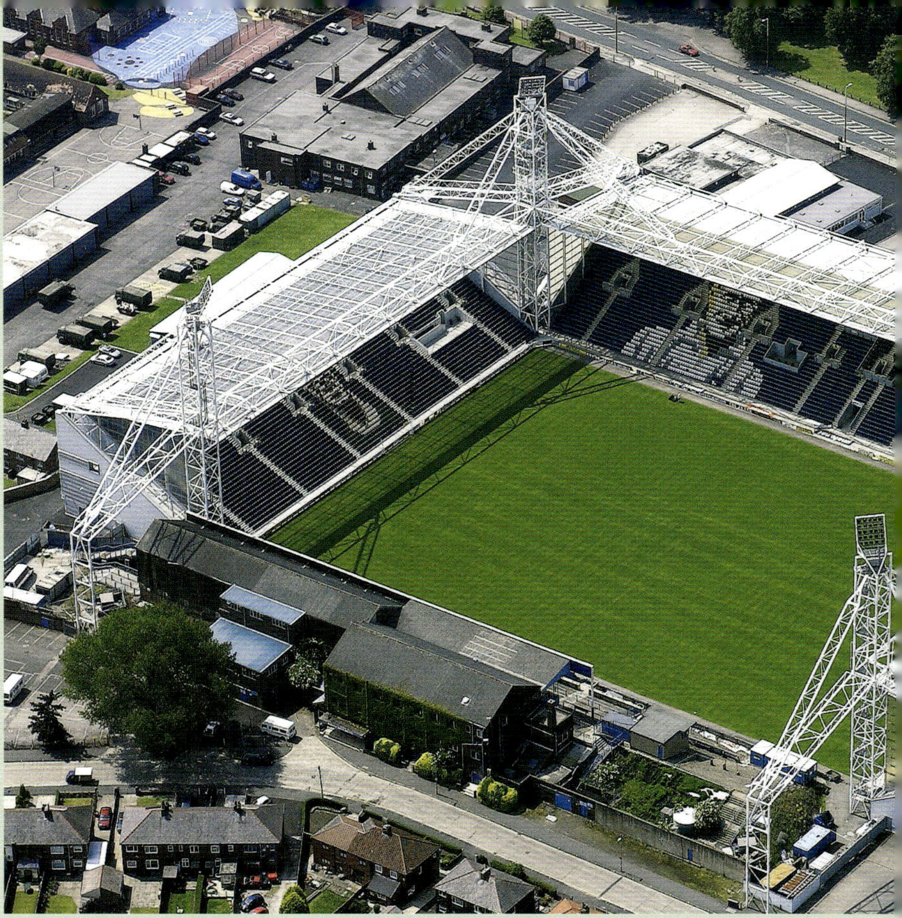

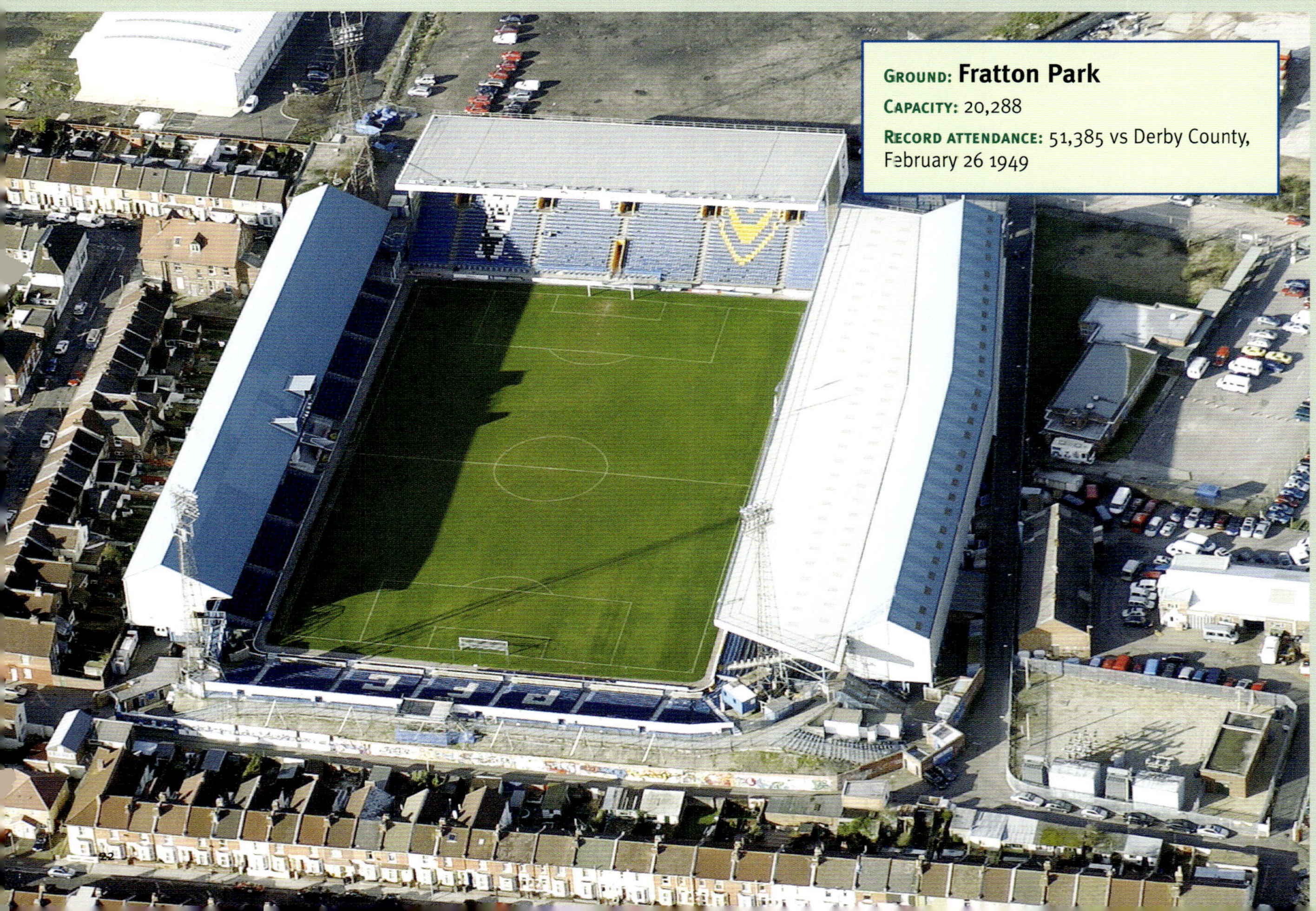

Ground: Fratton Park
Capacity: 20,288
Record attendance: 51,385 vs Derby County, February 26 1949

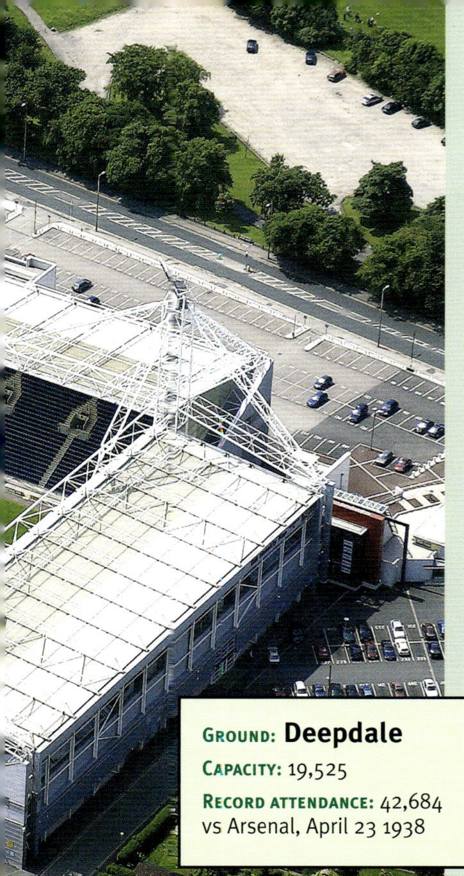

Ground: Deepdale
Capacity: 19,525
Record attendance: 42,684 vs Arsenal, April 23 1938

Preston North End

Preston North End was formed as North End Cricket Club in 1863. It moved to Deepdale in 1875. In 1878 the club played their first game of football. By this time, Deepdale had two stands on the west side and uncovered stands at the east and north ends. Preston were expelled from the Cup in 1884 after it was discovered they were paying their players and the Lilywhites formed Britain's first professional football team in 1885. In 1906 the Grandstand was opened and in 1921 a Kop was erected at the Fulwood Road End. During the 1930s a cover was added to the Town End, a pavilion was built along the east side and a second pavilion was erected on the south side in 1936. In 1996 the West Stand was replaced by a new single-tiered stand and a new stand was built where the North Terrace had once stood. The final stand to be replaced was the pavilion at the south end. The National Museum of Football is now located at Deepdale and is housed in two sides of the stadium.

Queens Park Rangers

Queens Park Rangers formed in 1882 from the old boys of Droop Street Board School. In 1886 the club took on the name Queens Park Rangers. QPR's first proper home was a waste ground near Kensal Rise Athletic Ground followed by a stint at Park Royal. In 1917 they moved to Loftus Road. They brought with them a stand and erected it on the south side. QPR left Loftus Road in 1930 due to crowd trouble. For two seasons they played at the White City. Crowds dropped and the large stadium lacked atmosphere, so the club returned to Loftus Road in 1933. In 1948 they bought the freehold of Loftus Road. However, the ground felt cramped and in 1962 the club moved back to the White City but returned once again to Loftus Road. A two-tier stand was built on the north side in 1966 and a new south stand opened in 1972. By 1981 there were two-tiered stands at either end and that year QPR unveiled the world's first artificial pitch, which remained until 1987 when it was replaced by grass.

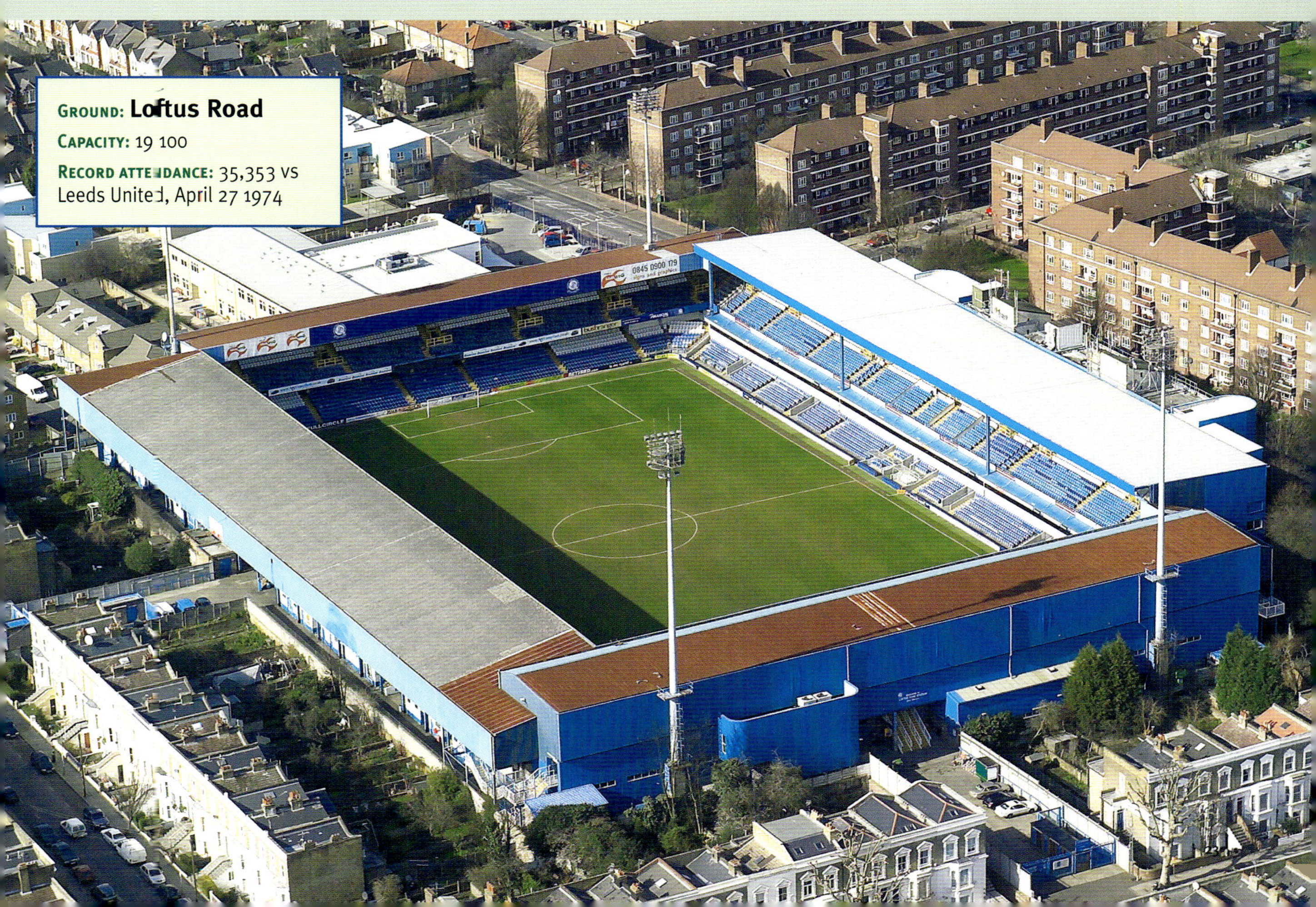

Ground: Loftus Road
Capacity: 19 100
Record attendance: 35,353 vs Leeds United, April 27 1974

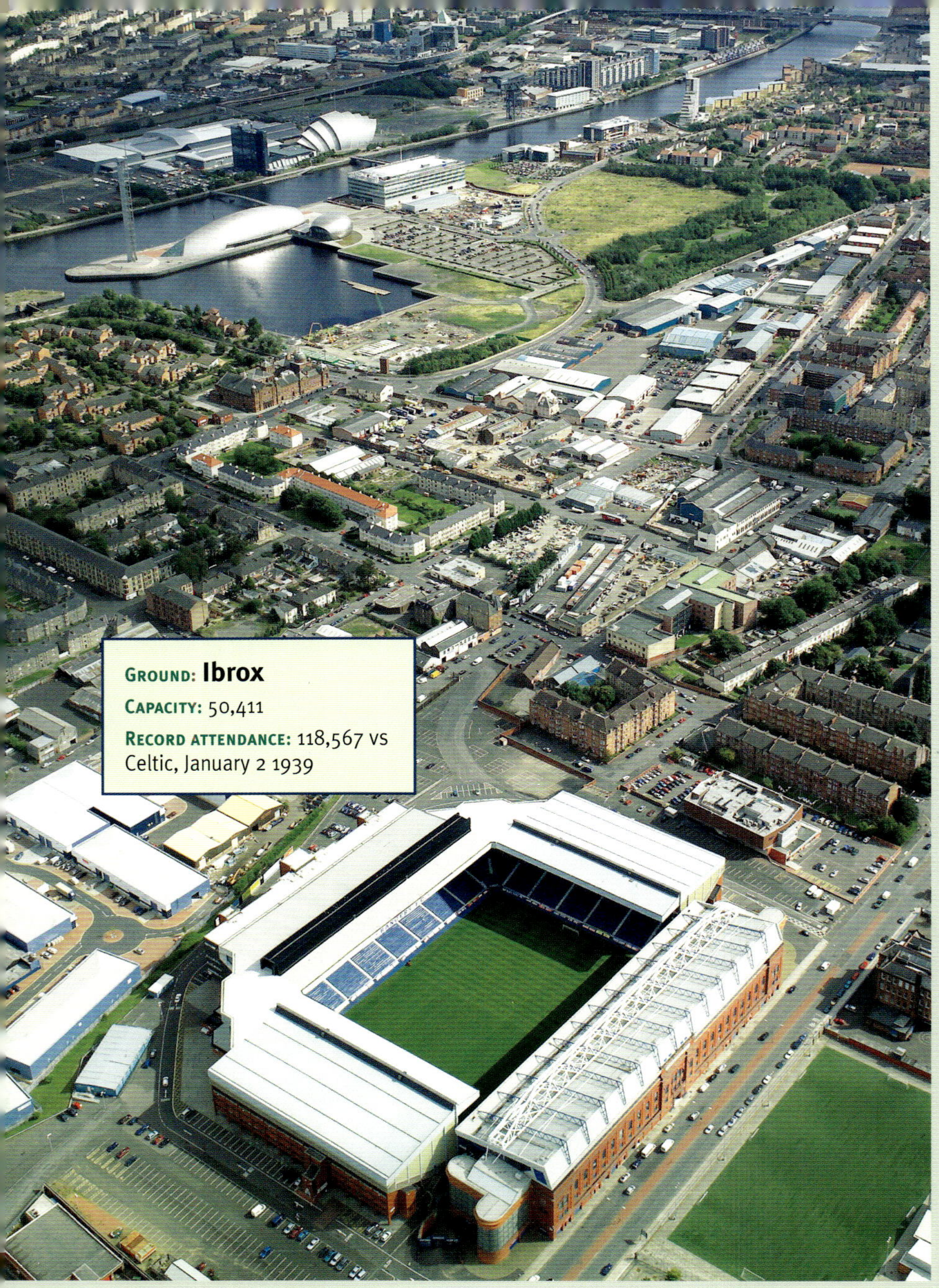

Ground: Ibrox
Capacity: 50,411
Record attendance: 118,567 vs Celtic, January 2 1939

Rangers

Rangers formed in 1873 and played their first games on Glasgow Green. They arrived at Ibrox in 1887 to a ground which borders their current stadium. In 1899, they built on the land next to their existing pitch. It had an oval track, a pavilion and a stand. In 1900 architect Archibald Leitch built terracing behind the west goal capable of holding 36,000. However, the terracing was unstable and in a game between England and Scotland in 1902 there was a tragic collapse, killing 26 and injuring 500. By 1910 Leitch had again been commissioned to expand Ibrox and increase its capacity to 63,000. Rangers won the League and Cup double in 1928 and this funded the building of the 10,000-seater double-decker South Stand. Tragedy struck again at Ibrox in 1971, when 66 people died and 145 were injured as the notorious Stairway 13 in the ground's north-east corner collapsed at the end of an Old Firm derby. Following the tragedy, the club rebuilt the ground except for Leitch's South Stand. The new Ibrox opened in 1981. David Murray took over in 1989 and another tier was added to the South Stand. The pitch was lowered by 12 inches in 1991 and the corners at either side of the Govan Stand completed in 1996.

Reading

Reading formed in 1871; in 1896 they left the flood-prone Caversham Cricket Ground for the drier option of Elm Park. When the Royals arrived, Elm Park had a small wooden main stand on the north side of the pitch and turfed terraces around the other three sides. In 1925 a cover, which had been added to offer protection over one of the terraces, blew down in a gale. In 1936 a roof was built over the terrace running along the south side of the ground. This roof was extended over both ends by the late 1950s. In the 1980s Elm Park needed investment. Some improvements were made but the club's proximity to local housing limited expansion. In 1990, businessman John Madejski stepped in with much needed funds. In 1998, Reading FC moved to the Madejski Stadium, an enclosed stadium with single-tiered stands on three sides and a two-tiered stand on the west side of the pitch. Expansion, adding extra tiers to the stands is planned soon.

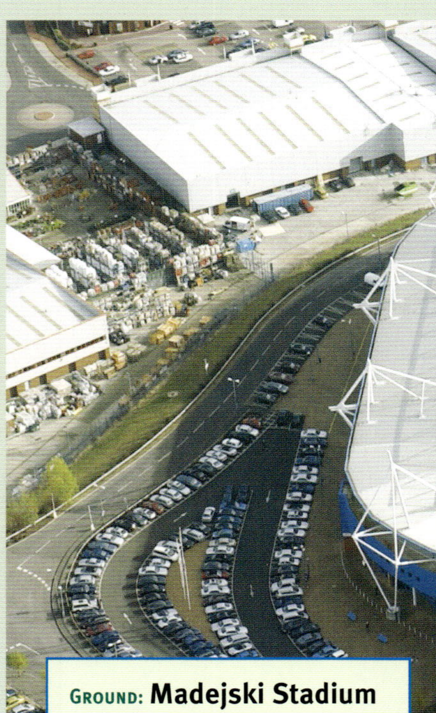

Ground: Madejski Stadium
Capacity: 24,200
Record attendance: (at Elm Park) 33,042 vs Brentford, February 19 1927
Record attendance: (at Madejski Stadium) 24,135 vs Manchester United, January 19 2008

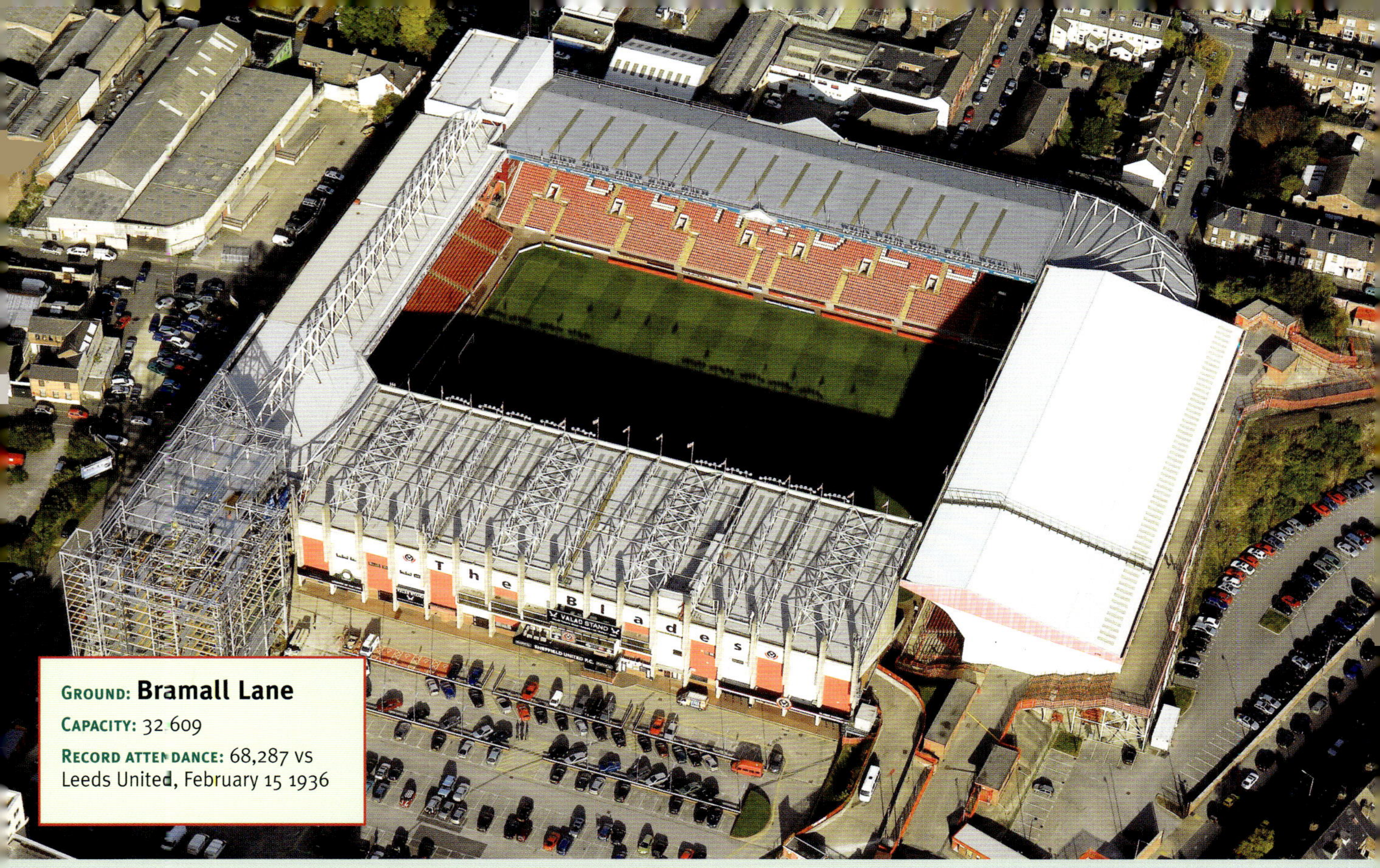

Ground: Bramall Lane
Capacity: 32 609
Record attendance: 68,287 vs Leeds United, February 15 1936

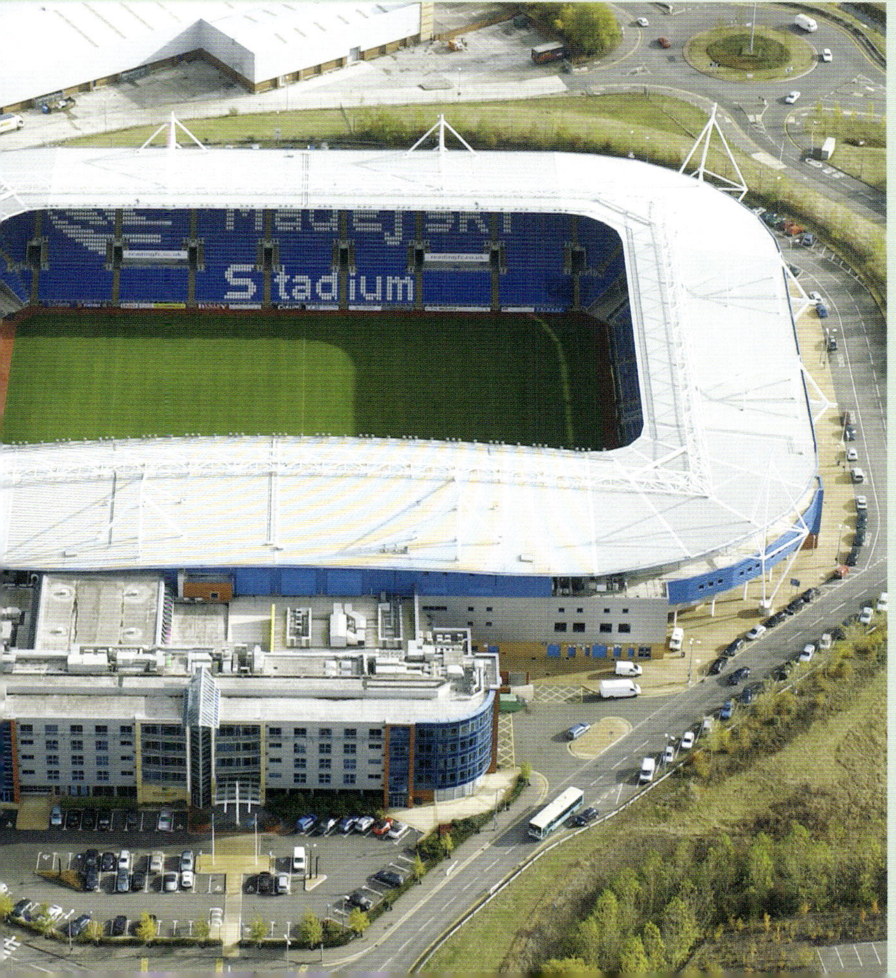

Sheffield United

Sheffield United first played at Bramall Lane in 1862 when Hallam FC took on Sheffield FC, the world's oldest football club. The ground was originally used however by Sheffield United Cricket Club from 1854. It was not until 1889 that Sheffield United Football Club formed. Success was rapid; in 1892 they were elected to the Second Division, earning promotion just a year later and winning their only League championship in 1898. Two stands were built at this time, at the Shoreham Street End and on John Street. In 1902 the John Street Stand replaced the earlier one that had been gutted by fire. Just before the First World War terracing was extended along the Bramall Lane End, known to fans as the Kop. A roof was added in 1935. Bramall Lane was bombed 10 times during WWII, damaging the John Street Stand, the Kop roof and the pitch. It took until 1954 to replace the John Street Stand. The South Stand opened in 1975. The 1990s saw further development of the ground. The John Street Stand was demolished in 1994 and a new stand opened in 1996.

Sheffield Wednesday

was established in 1867 as the football playing section of Wednesday Cricket Club. The club played at various grounds before severing ties with the cricket club and moving to Olive Grove in 1887. The lease of the ground ended in 1898 and Wednesday found themselves homeless. In 1899 the club moved to a ground in Owlerton bringing with them the Main Stand from Olive Grove. In 1913 the Spion Kop and the South Stand were built. The club changed the ground's name to Hillsborough in 1914. A cantilevered grandstand, the North Stand, capable of seating 9,882 fans, replaced the Olive Grove Stand in 1961. Hillsborough staged some of the games in the 1966 World Cup, so Wednesday built the new West Stand and added seats to the South Stand paddock. On April 15 1989 the ground saw its darkest day when 96 Liverpool fans were crushed to death. The subsequent Taylor report required all top clubs in England, Wales and Scotland to become all-seater. The Owls spent £10m on improvements, adding seats to the South Stand, the lower tier of the West Stand and the Kop.

Southampton

formed in 1885 and were called Southampton St Mary's FC. They played their first games on the site of the County Bowling Club and then moved to the Antelope Cricket Ground. They turned professional in 1894. Two years later they changed their name to Southampton FC and in 1898 moved to The Dell. A local fish merchant, George Thomas, funded the development of the ground. Both ends were terraced and stands were erected on the east and west sides. The club won promotion in 1922 and were able to expand the ground, beginning with an extension of the East Stand. In 1927/8 the new West Stand was erected. In the late 1940s three concrete platforms known as the chocolate boxes were fixed above the Milton Road End terrace. The Taylor report reduced the ground's capacity and by the late 1980s the club began to look for a larger site. In August 2001, the new £32m all-seater St Mary's Stadium was opened on the site of a former gasworks.

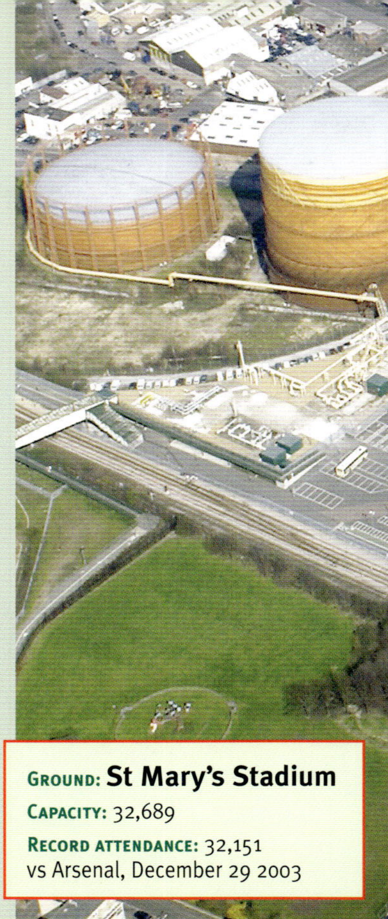

Ground: **St Mary's Stadium**
Capacity: 32,689
Record attendance: 32,151 vs Arsenal, December 29 2003

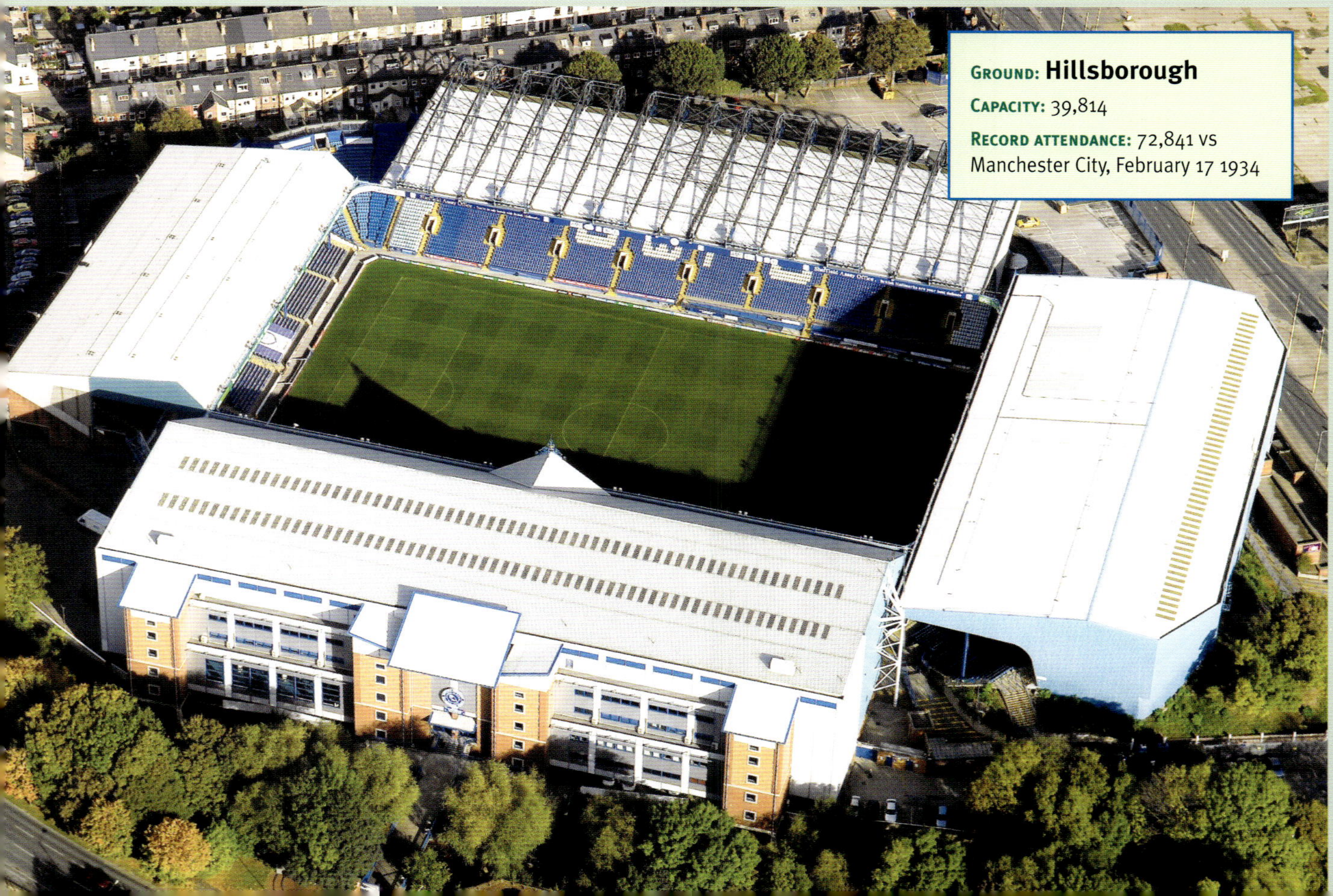

Ground: **Hillsborough**
Capacity: 39,814
Record attendance: 72,841 vs Manchester City, February 17 1934

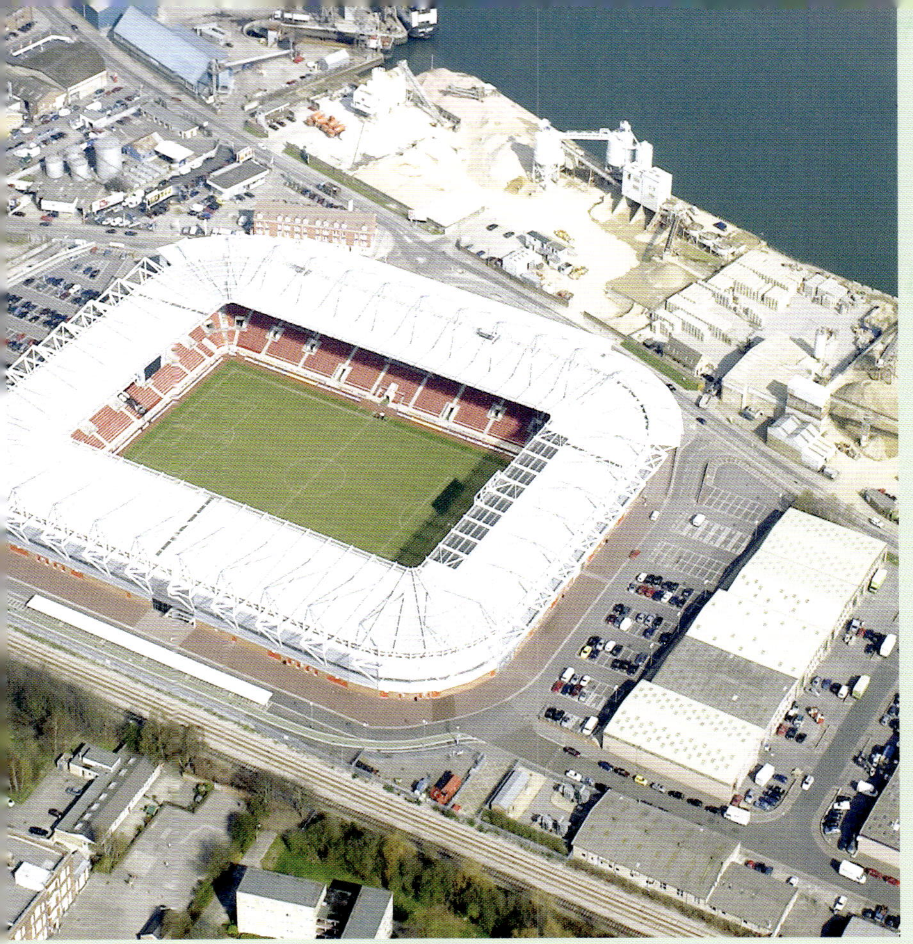

Sunderland played their first games at Blue House field. They moved four times before settling at Newcastle Road. The new ground was already enclosed on three sides, so the club only had to build one further stand on the east side to complete the work. In 1898 the club moved to Roker Park, where it stayed for 99 years. During the summer two stands were built – the Grandstand and the Clock Stand; the other two ends were left open. The 1920s saw further developments; in 1925 the Fulwell End was expanded bringing capacity to 60,000 and the Main Stand was erected in 1929. The Clock Stand was replaced in 1936. Roker Park was selected as a World Cup venue and the pitch was expanded by 3 yards while seats were added in the Clock Stand and the Fulwell End was covered. In 1997 the club moved to a new site at the former Monkwearmouth Colliery. The ground has three two-tier stands on the north, south and east sides linking to the Main Stand on the west.

Ground: **Stadium of Light**

Capacity 49,000

Record attendance: (at Roker Park) 75,118 vs Derby County, March 8 1933

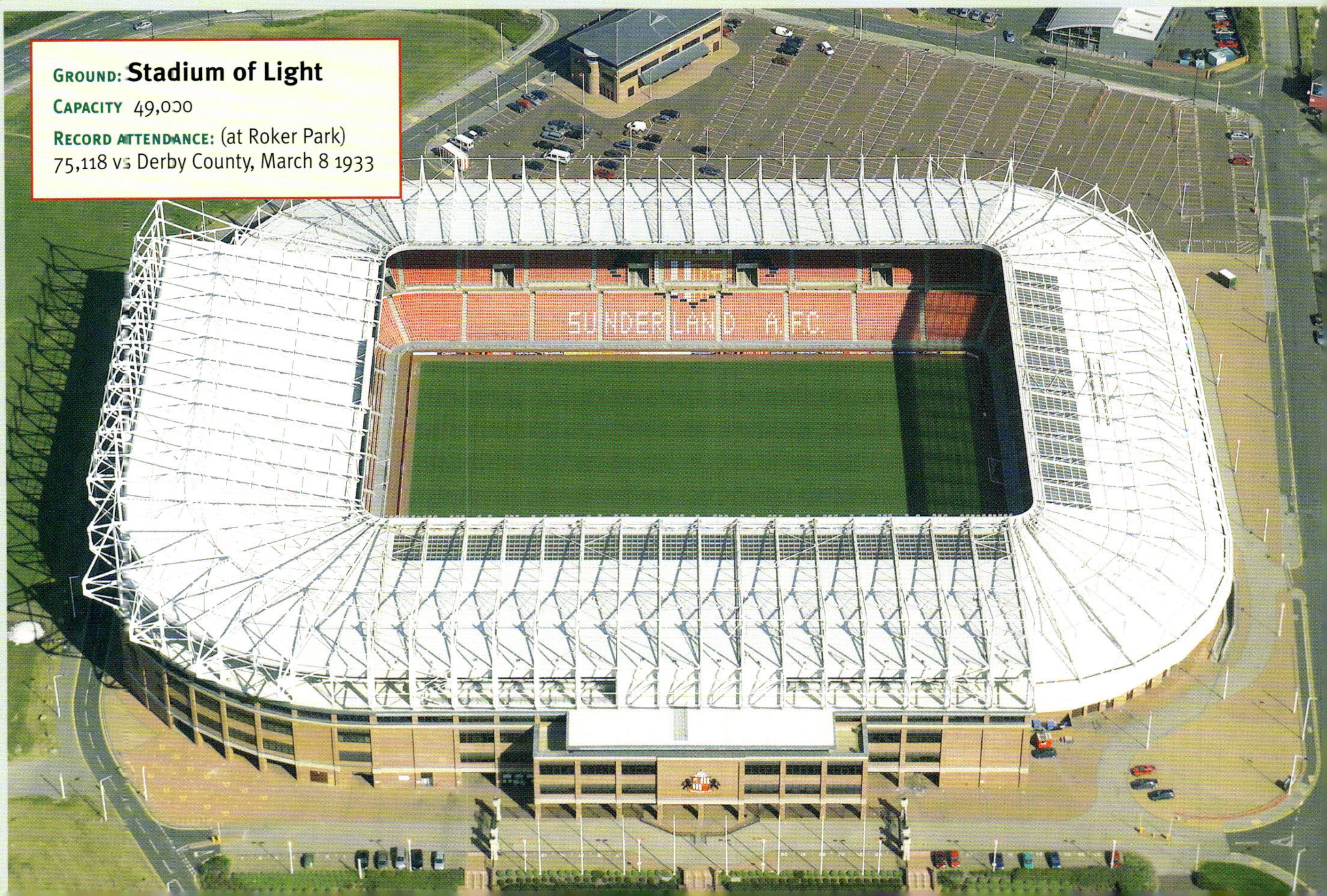

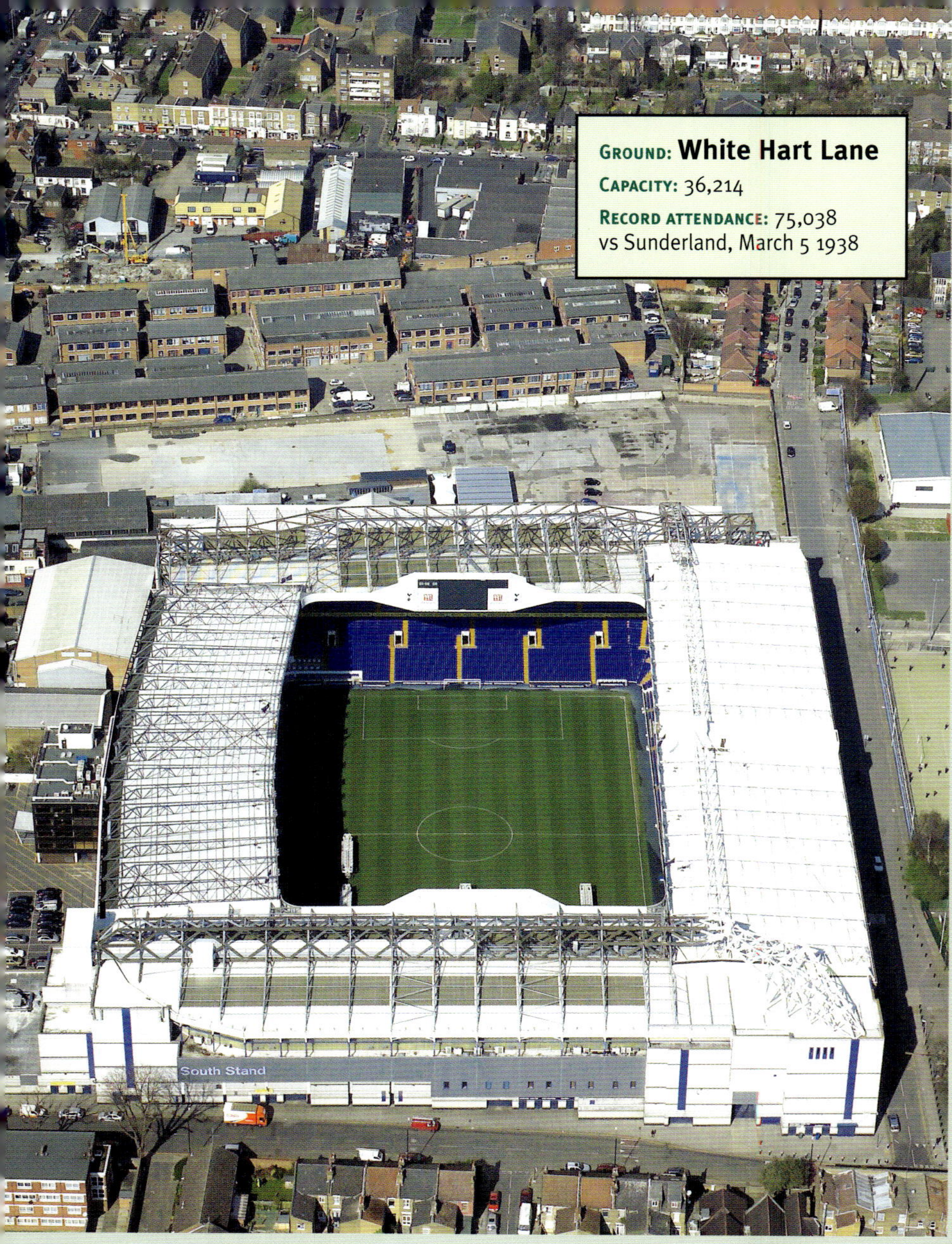

Ground: White Hart Lane
Capacity: 36,214
Record attendance: 75,038 vs Sunderland, March 5 1938

Tottenham Hotspur was formed by a group of cricketers in 1882. The team, then called Hotspur FC, first played games on Tottenham Marshes. By 1885, the club had added the prefix "Tottenham" and three years later moved to their first ground, Northumberland Park. In 1899 the club moved again to a ground owned by a local brewery then called the High Road Ground. The club's first major stand, the West Stand, was opened in 1909. The stand came complete with a mock-Tudor gable and a year later a copper cockerel perched on a ball was placed on the roof. In 1919 the ground adopted the name of the local station – White Hart Lane. It was not until 1934 that the final terrace – the East Terrace – was built. The East Stand was a two-tier stand erected on top of the terracing. The cockerel moved to the East Stand in 1958, in time to see the club go through their most successful era. In the 1980s, the club nearly went bankrupt as the building of the West Stand cost almost double the original estimated fee. The redevelopment of the East Stand in 1987 again caused crippling debt as costs spiralled. However, the club managed its debts and after adding seats to the East Terrace, the Park Lane Terrace and the Shelf, the new South Stand was built in 1995, and a new upper tier was added to the Paxton Road End.

Wembley The first Wembley Stadium was a project devised by the government in 1918 in the aftermath of the First World War. Plans were drawn up for a British Empire Exhibition with a national sporting stadium as its centrepiece. It was originally named the Empire Stadium, designed by architects Sir John Simpson and Maxwell Ayerton; it took just 300 days to complete. George V officially opened the Empire Exhibition in 1924, although the first event held at the stadium was the 1923 Cup Final

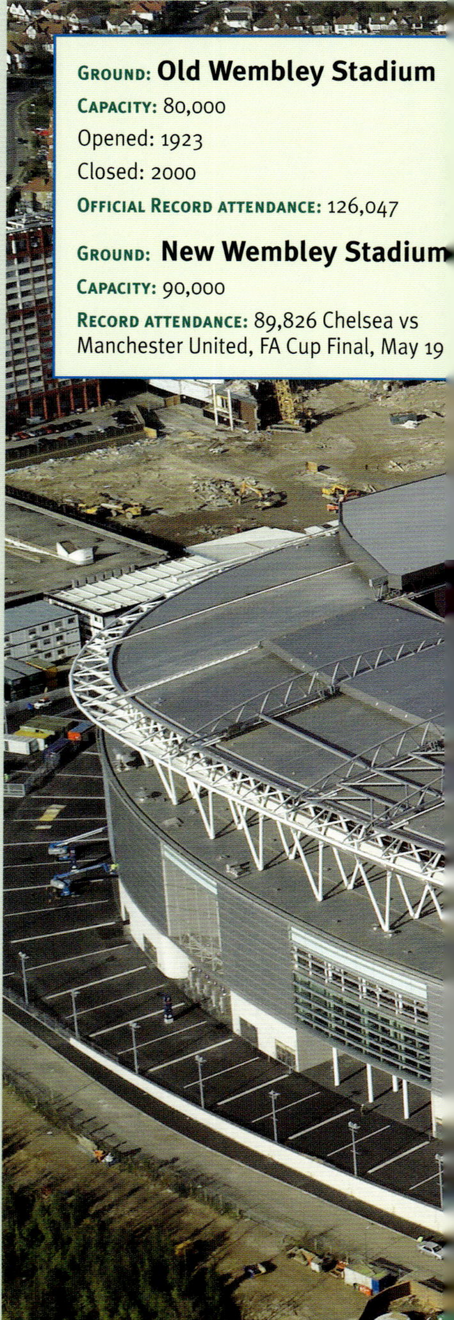

Ground: Old Wembley Stadium
Capacity: 80,000
Opened: 1923
Closed: 2000
Official Record attendance: 126,047

Ground: New Wembley Stadium
Capacity: 90,000
Record attendance: 89,826 Chelsea vs Manchester United, FA Cup Final, May 19

between West Ham United and Bolton Wanderers. During that game the stadium's official capacity of 126,047 was far exceeded and an estimated 200,000 people crammed in to see the game. Spectators spilled onto the pitch and the game became known as the "white horse final" because newsreel film captured the memorable sight of a policeman on a white horse vainly trying to clear the pitch. At this time, the ground was oval-shaped and the pitch was surrounded by a running track. The north and south ends of the stadium had seated stands, while the remaining sides had open terracing. Floodlights were added to the stadium in 1955 and the encircling roof and electronic scoreboards were added in 1963. In 1990, following the Taylor report, the ground became all-seater and had a capacity of 80,000. Apart from these developments, very little changed in Wembley's structure from its original 1920s design. However, its poor facilities, coupled with its difficult access, led to calls for Wembley to be rebuilt. The first Wembley Stadium was finally closed in 2000 and demolition of the buildings began. The iconic twin towers came down in December 2002.

The new Wembley Stadium was completed in March 2007 and the first Cup final, between Manchester United and Chelsea, played on May 19 2007. The ground has cost an estimated £760m to redevelop and boasts a fully retractable roof and an eye-catching arch, visible all over London. In 2012 the new Wembley Stadium will host the football competition as part of the London Olympics.

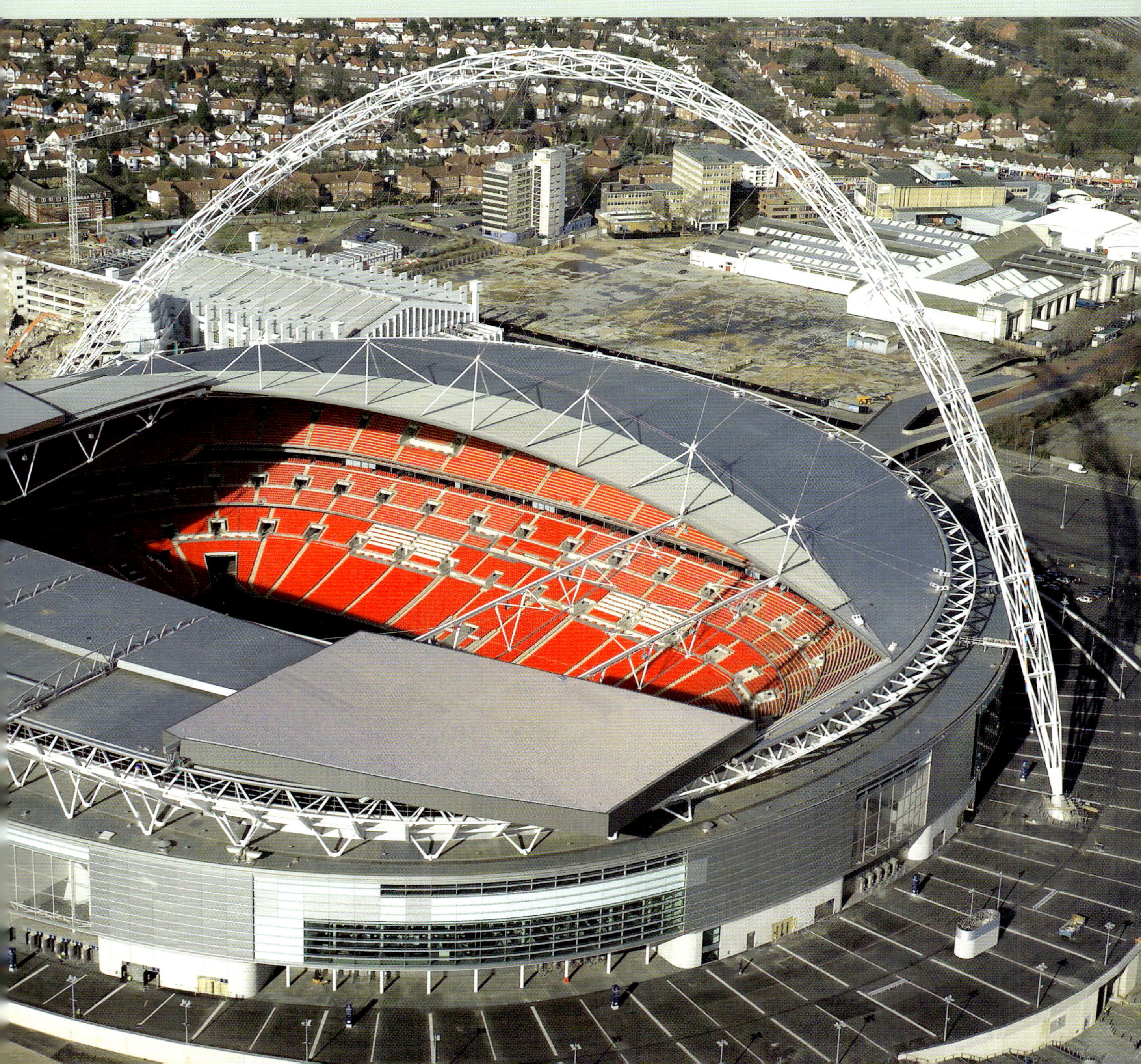

Watford

Watford can trace its roots back to 1881 and a team called Watford Rovers. Rovers played at Cassiobury Park before moving to Rose and Crown Park, followed by a stint at Colney Butts Meadow. The club changed their name to West Herts in 1891 and moved to the West Herts Sports Ground. In 1922 Watford moved to Vicarage Road, a former gravel pit. The Hornets built a new 3,500-seater main stand. A large embankment was built at the north end. In 1928 the club introduced greyhound racing to Vicarage Road. After the Second World War, Watford added a roof to the south end. In 1976 long-time fan Elton John became chairman and Graham Taylor took over as manager. In 1986 the Hornets' chairman opened a brand new two-tiered stand, the Rous Stand, on the west side of the ground. During the 1990s the Hornets built new, single-tiered stands at either end and further developed the front of the Rous Stand.

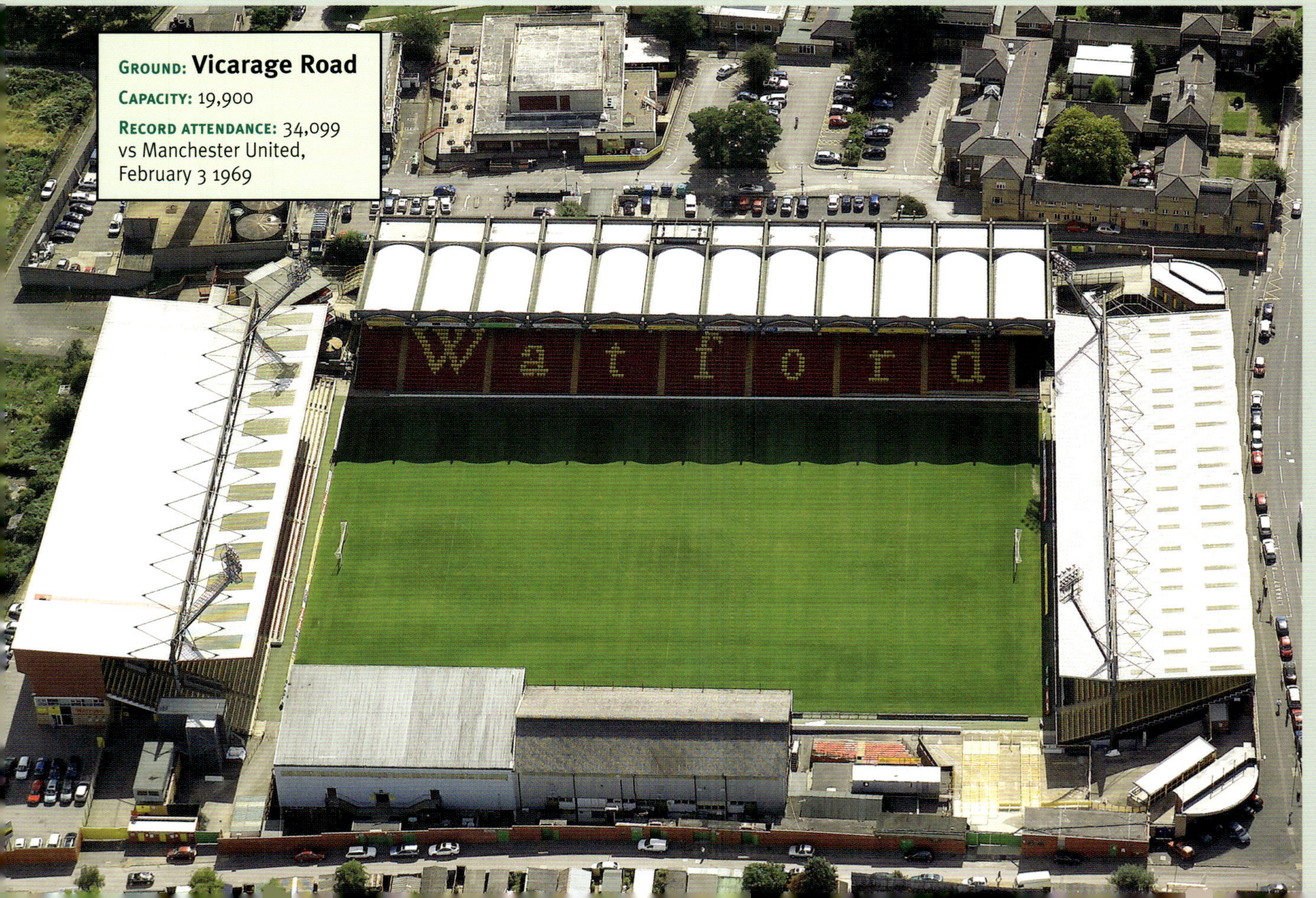

Ground: Vicarage Road
Capacity: 19,900
Record attendance: 34,099 vs Manchester United, February 3 1969

West Bromwich Albion

West Bromwich Albion was created by a group of workers from Salter's Spring Works in 1878. They originally called themselves the West Bromwich Strollers after walking to nearby Wednesbury to buy a ball. The name stuck until 1880, when they changed their name to the more familiar Albion. The club played at five different grounds before settling at the Hawthorns in 1900, so-called because the ground was once surrounded by hawthorn bushes. The initial capacity was 35,500 but when the club bought the ground's freehold in 1913 it began developing the stands. In 1931 terracing was completed on all four sides of the ground. The more familiar stands of today were constructed between the 1940s and the 1960s. The East Stand, known as the Rainbow Stand because of its multi-coloured seats, was built on the site of the former Handsworth Stand. Following the Taylor report, a new stadium was opened in 1995. The Rainbow Stand was finally demolished in 2001 to make way for the new East Stand.

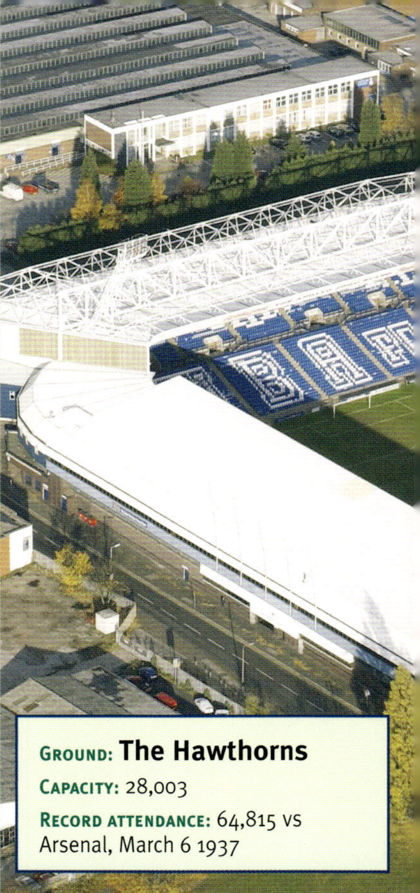

Ground: The Hawthorns
Capacity: 28,003
Record attendance: 64,815 vs Arsenal, March 6 1937

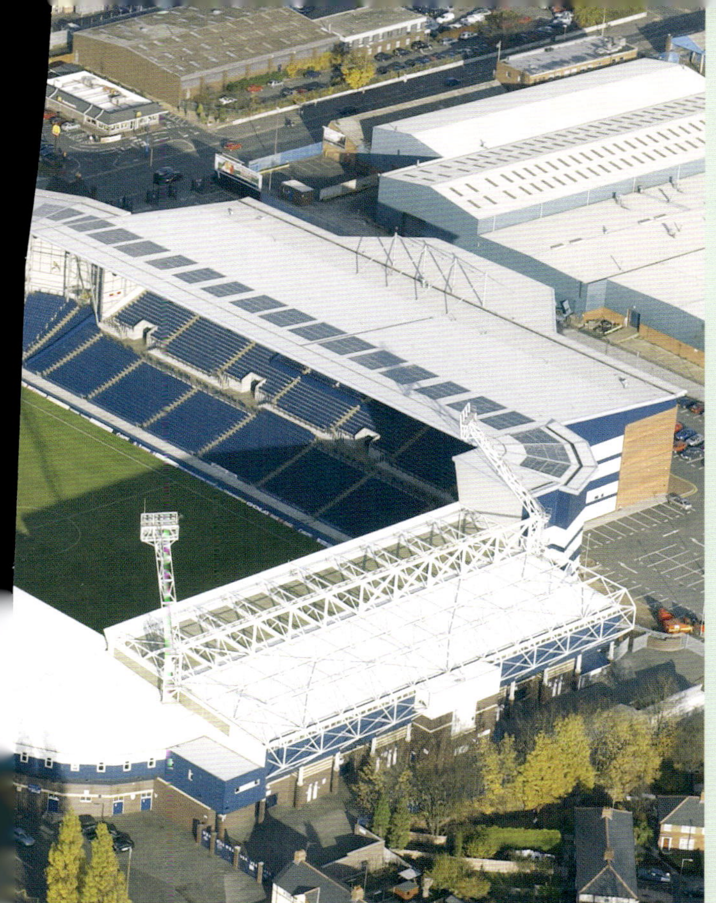

West Ham United began as Thames Ironworks, a team set up by Arnold Hills in 1895. Hills was a shipyard owner and the club's nickname, the Hammers, refers to the tools used by shipyard workers. The team originally played at Hermit Road in Canning Town before eventually moving to Upton Park in 1904, four years after renaming themselves West Ham United. The club's ground is called the Boleyn Ground, named after a 16th-century house that stood next door to the ground. Attendances climbed and in 1913 the new West Stand was built, which was extended in 1925 to a two-tier structure. During this time the South Stand was covered, as was the East Stand. The Second World War saw severe damage to the South Stand when a V1 bomb landed on the ground. Another bay was added to the West Stand and the East Stand was completely rebuilt, significantly raising capacity. As with many other clubs, the ground had to reduce its capacity following the Taylor report. In 1991, the club bought land behind the West Stand, which they rebuilt and expanded. Financial problems and boycotts saw gates drop below 16,000. To try and lure fans back, the club slashed the price of season tickets and eventually began redeveloping the South Stand (now the Centenary Stand) in 1993. The Bobby Moore Stand opened in 1994, the new millennium brought further redevelopments to the Dr Marten's Stand and the East Stand.

Ground: **Upton Park**

Capacity: 35,146

Record attendance: 42,322 vs Tottenham Hotspur, October 17 1970

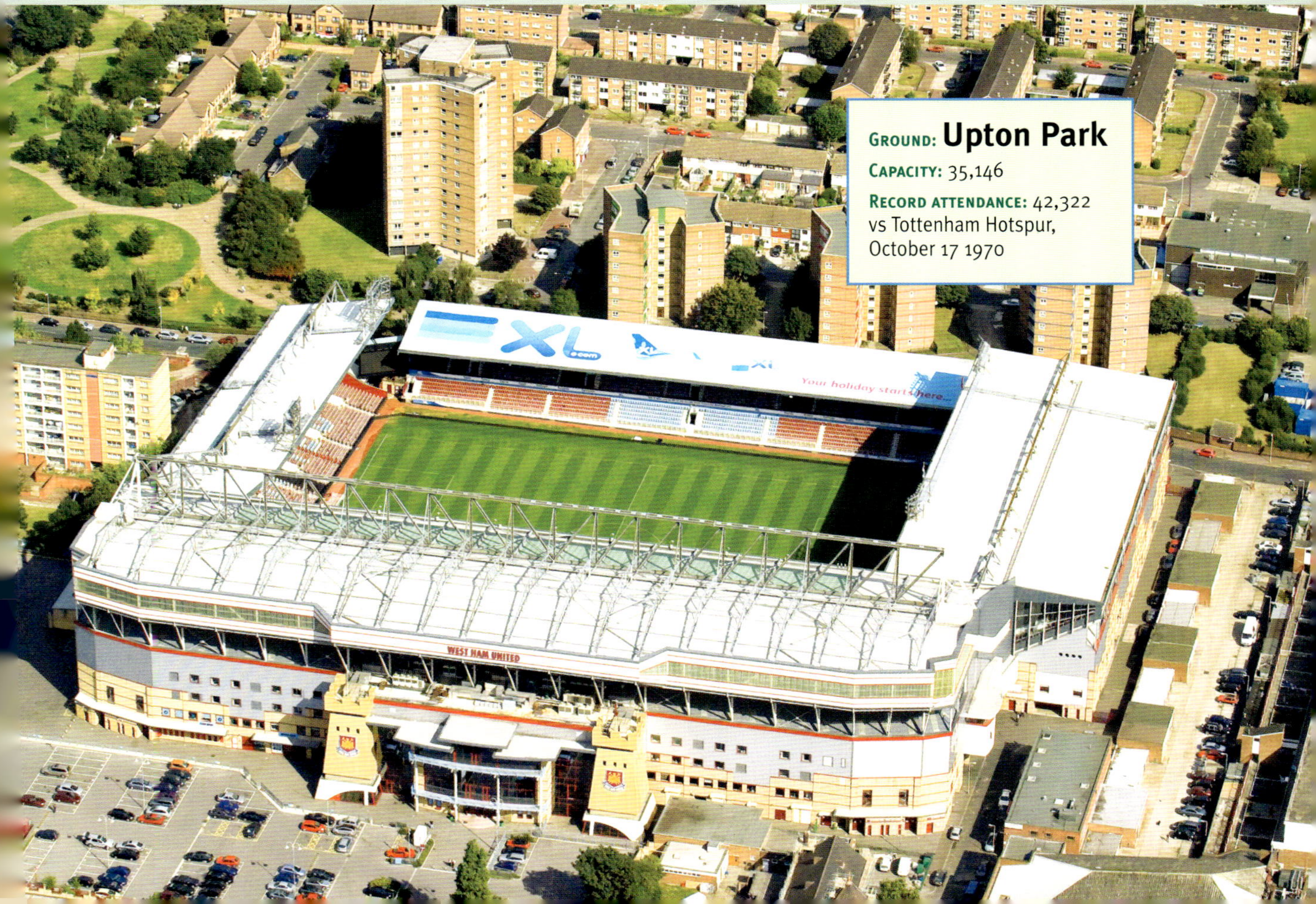

Wigan Springfield Park, Wigan's original home ground, was first used for football in 1897 by Wigan County. Before then the ground was a sports ground with a horse trotting track, a concrete cycle track and a running track. Following Wigan County's demise, a succession of Wigan clubs formed and disbanded, Wigan Borough being the most successful, lasting from 1919 to 1932. During Borough's ownership of the ground the original stands were replaced and the new Main Stand created. The Shevington End Stand and the Popular Side Stand were also constructed during this period. When Wigan Athletic formed in 1932, they bought Springfield Park and this remained the Latics' home for the next 67 years. The Latics' first game at Springfield Park was against Port Vale Reserves, which ended in a 2-0 defeat for the home side. The club fought for League status until 1978. During this time they drew the largest crowd in their history. The Latics finally made it in to the League after 34 attempts in 1978. They marked the occasion by losing 3-0 to Grimsby Town. The Latics had mixed success after joining the league. An impressive start saw them promoted to the Third Division at the end of the 1981-82 season. They stared bankruptcy and relegation to the Conference in the face after a bad run of results in the 1992/3 season, but their fortunes were reversed when businessman Dave Whelan bought the club in 1995. He financed the building of the new JJB Stadium, which they moved to in 1999. The new stadium is shared with local rugby league team Wigan Warriors, also owned by Whelan, who moved from Central Park in 1999.

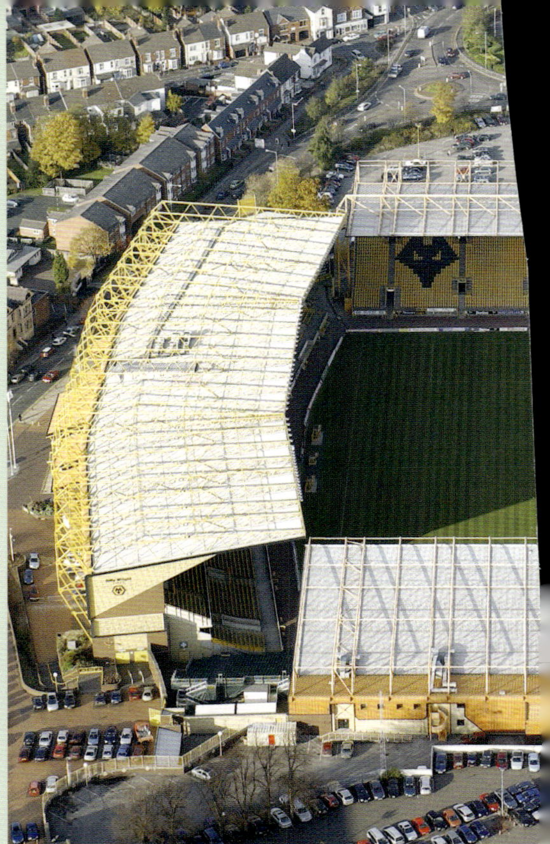

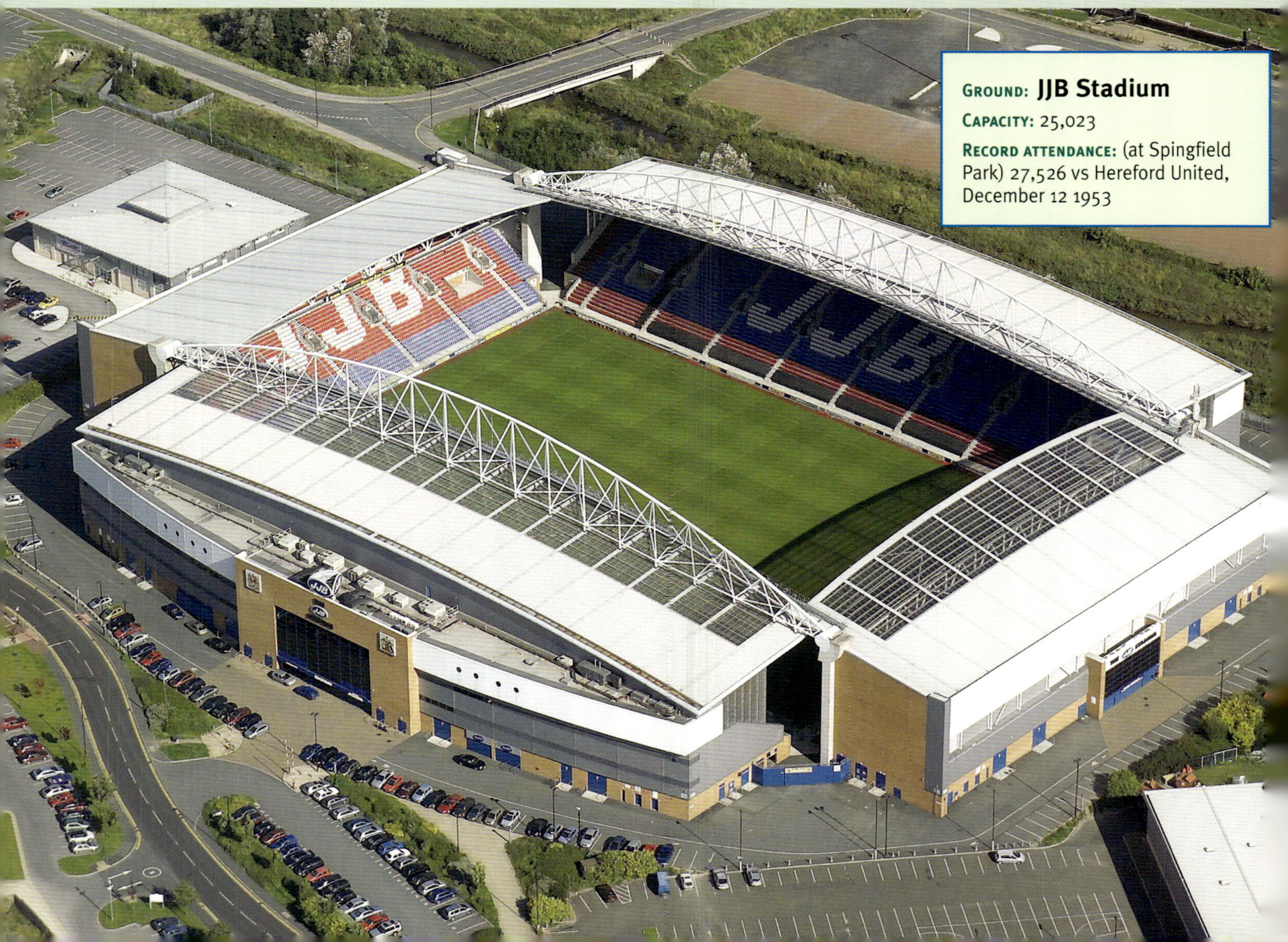

GROUND: JJB Stadium

CAPACITY: 25,023

RECORD ATTENDANCE: (at Spingfield Park) 27,526 vs Hereford United, December 12 1953